CW00530248

STANTON WILLIAMS

VOLUME

£8

black dog publishing

london uk

Contents

(Cover) *When the workers take the stone out... they are putting space inside the mountain... I realised that I could have the space and they could have the stone.* Eduardo Chillida

The architecture and design practice Stanton Williams was founded in 1985 by Alan Stanton and Paul Williams. The London-based studio now has a team of over 50 people with five directors and six associates.

Stanton Williams has completed over 350 architectural, urban design, masterplanning, exhibition and interior design projects, winning more than 50 awards, in the arts, culture, education, retail, commerce, residential development and local government.

STARTING AT THE BEGINNING

Starting at the Beginning
Irénée Scalbert

If it did exist, a typical Stanton Williams image might look something like this. A wall fills most of the frame, it is viewed head-on and it is painted white. Perhaps a tall window slits the wall in halves, affording light rather than a view. Probably, an architectural element intrudes into the frame, for example a glass balustrade capped with the line of a handrail, or the stainless string of a stairs rising along the wall. Certainly, a beam of light falls diagonally across the wall, its source out of sight. This image is not a demonstration of the magnificent play of volumes under the light dear to Le Corbusier. It is instead an instance of the delicate play of light in space. It conveys a sensitive mood, a distinctive calm and an inviting absence. And it does not lend itself to a ready-made definition.

Alan Stanton and Paul Williams regard themselves not as ideologues but as makers, as craftsmen putting things together in ways that need only few words. This was not born out of a desire to encourage a more ascetic life—unlike some of their contemporaries, they have shown no monastic or minimalist aspirations. More simply, their work is the expression of a practical sensibility. If there were a frustration with the practice of architecture, it would be that design can never be concrete enough, that it often remains bound by the limitations of card models and geometrical planes. Stanton and Williams have claimed to see architecture with the eye of sculptors. They are never more at ease than when making things or witnessing the fabrication of things in a workshop or a factory.

Were there to be an overarching Stanton Williams project, it might find an echo in a 1924 text by van Doesburg, aptly titled "Towards a Plastic Architecture". Its author insists that there can be in architecture no basic type, therefore no basis for replication or imitation. He evokes an elemental architecture made with the most basic elements of design: with function, mass, surface, time, space, light, colour, material.[1] Stanton Williams might further feel sympathy with Piet Mondrian who contemplated a horizon beyond which the environment, no longer separate from art, will consist in a unified plastic reality. Stanton Williams do in fact acknowledge a debt to de Stijl, more particularly in their early exhibition designs.

Occasionally, resemblances can be found with works by Carlo Scarpa and Louis Kahn, discovered by Williams while a student, with Wright perhaps (Williams' first job after graduation was to reassemble Edgar Kaufmann's office at the Victoria and Albert Museum), and with Rudolf Schindler, a self-declared 'space architect'. But unlike contemporaries associated with the 9H magazine and gallery in the 1980s, they showed no urgency to absorb the formal language of other architects, of Adolf Loos, Mies van der Rohe and Álvaro Siza, of Tadao Ando, Luigi Snozzi and Luis Barragán. Whatever familiarity Stanton Williams may have with these architects, this is not their way.

Stanton Williams are modern architects. They are modern because, being first and foremost plasticians, they continue the line of research in materials and in forms initiated at the Bauhaus. 1934 could serve as a symbolic date for a critical genealogy of their work. László Moholy-Nagy had arrived in London. His main book *The New Vision,* based on his preliminary course at the Bauhaus, had been published in English. Ben Nicholson had carved his first bas-reliefs, and he had met Piet Mondrian in Paris. The art critic Herbert Read ("art is an attempt to create pleasing forms") was a friend of Nicholson. So was Adrian Stokes who had formulated in the previous year a theory about the signification of carving in art.[2] The Hampstead crowd of which they were a part was cosmopolitan but English. All wished to scrutinise the fundamentals of artistic practice. They desired, in the words used by Nicholson about himself, "to get right back to the beginning and then take one step forward at a time on a firm basis".[3] These words describe equally well the intentions of Stanton Williams some 50 years later.

Stanton worked with Renzo Piano and Richard Rogers on the Pompidou Centre for seven years. His last two years on the project had a significant impact on his later views on architecture. The team had started work on the interiors. Pontus Hulten, the new director of the Musée National d'Art Moderne, imagined a 'museum-village' in which key works were presented in 'squares', and art movements, in 'cabanes' or huts dispersed across the open floor. The design team had different ideas. Stanton sought a solution in scale with the vast floor of the centre. He looked at photographs of Mies van der Rohe's National Gallery in Berlin and at his famous collage in which large paintings floated, de Stijl-like, in a vast industrial space. In this way the large spaces of the Pompidou Centre, dominated by trusses that take up half the depth of floors (and whose impact noone had considered), might be tamed.

Hulten won the argument and the result was a compromise. He got his huts made with floating walls and ceiling that fell just short of touching one another. The art, the walls and the space, Stanton recalls, were struggling. The disappointment was a turning point, leading him to realise how much was lacking in terms of the character and the quality of the spaces. In hindsight, he regards this interior as the inverse of Stanton Williams' work: "we start," he says, "with the things which the Pompidou Centre did not address".[4] In the Pompidou Centre, structure and systems dominate the space; in the work of Stanton Williams, internal space drives the design, structure being rarely expressed and remaining for the most part out of sight.

Stanton then looked for a new start. Modern architecture had so fetishised technology and rationality that considerations relating to actual experience became secondary—this was the lesson of the Musée d'Art Moderne. In the late 1970s, priorities were reversed: the experience of forms and the capacity to find meaning in them prevailed. Oddly, this conclusion to which Stanton arrived after several years of questioning and exploring was consistent with the fundamental Bauhaus values that Williams had inherited. As Stanton recalls, Williams was coming "from the other side"—other from the one that the Pompidou Centre had represented. In his work as an exhibition designer, he was in constant contact with fabricators, with materials and with actual spaces. Unlike many architects who became hostage to the process which they set in motion, he was proceeding as it were from the inside outwards, from the object to the space, from the small to the large, enabling him to be fully in control of the design.

Williams had been studying art in Birmingham. Two exhibitions in London, both of 1968, made a lasting impression: Cybernetic Serendipity at the ICA which included Moholy-Nagy's film *Light Play: Black-White-Grey*, and above all Bauhaus: 50 years at the Royal Academy, the catalogue of which became Williams' "bible for many years". Within the large body of work of the Bauhaus, Williams makes no mention of Walter Gropius, Mies van der Rohe or Hannes Meyer. The artists, especially Moholy-Nagy, stood out, and it is not difficult to see why. Moholy-Nagy's dedication to achieving a "mastery of the surface… for plastic, spatial ends", his use of light in lieu of pigments in photograms, his "step by step articulation of the material", his conception of space as "the reality of sensory experience": there is much in Moholy-Nagy that resonates with the light-sensitive interiors of Stanton Williams.[5]

Williams' first job after leaving University was in the Design Studio of the V&A in London. There he worked directly under its then director, Roy Strong, who put a new emphasis upon temporary exhibitions. Exhibition design was the preserve of a small number of practitioners including architects Michael Brawne, Neave Brown and Alan Irvine, who had worked with Carlo Scarpa. Scarpa who was little known at the time outside Italy save for his exhibition designs, was perhaps the only architect to have left a stylistic mark on Williams. While still at the V&A Williams was awarded a research grant to study museum and gallery design in USA, before setting up his own practice in 1979. Soon Williams was designing exhibitions worldwide.

The influence of Scarpa was perhaps most evident in one of Williams' best remembered shows at the Hayward Gallery in London, the Romanesque exhibition of 1984. It was praised by the art critic David Sylvester, who said that "he had never seen a show that was better designed at once imaginative in conception and perfect in detail".[6] The galleries were orchestrated by folding and floating wall planes, and carefully staged vistas focused on objects that helped to draw visitors through a succession of dramatically lit contrasting gallery spaces. Williams took down the tattered black muslin below the ceiling (installed, ironically by Scarpa for the show Frescoes from Florence in 1969), and he exposed the concrete walls and staircases hidden by layers of chipboard linings. Romanesque works were enhanced by the Brutalist setting and the show helped to restore faith in the Hayward Gallery that was then threatened with closure.

By 1985, when Stanton and Williams established their office, both had accumulated considerable experience in exhibition design and much of their early work was in this field. This formative experience is reflected in the later work: the mood of concentration, the emphasis on interiors, the spatial composition by means of distinct, interlocking elements, and the essential presence ascribed not to objects of course but to individuals. It is reflected, too, in details that accentuate the materiality, the texture, even on occasions the weight of elements. At the same time, they achieve a sense of fluidity, of continuity and of lightness. They are drawn with considerable precision, yet (unlike Scarpa's) they mostly escape attention, as if the architects had gently rubbed over them with an eraser. Seldom in architecture do details contribute so much to the mood of the space. Details are in Stanton Williams' work a major, sometimes the principal source of spatial expression, yet they are consistently underplayed.

This approach is visible in a corner detail at the Compton Verney Art Gallery. The gallery, grafted on an eighteenth century mansion, is in effect Stanton Williams' own Castelvecchio (Stanton Williams worked on the project for 11 years, only three years less than Scarpa did in Verona). As you walk through the entrance into the new extension, in the far corner of the inevitable bookshop, a clerestory window affords a view of ancillary buildings beyond. Standing outside the extension, you are made aware of its simple volume, seemingly carved in a single block of limestone. At the point where one most expects the block to sit firmly in the landscape, corresponding to the bookshop clerestory inside, contact with the ground is denied. All the effort is concentrated on the suppression of the unavoidable column. The weight of the block, which is at this point considerable, is channelled through the corner mullion of the window. Especially felicitous is the turning of the L-shaped mullion outwards, the short projecting flange further contributing to the denial of both corner and weight.

In the mansion, the new details step back, sometimes literally, within the existing fabric. For instance, in the room accommodating the new entrance, the issue was how to make a door-opening leading to the extension in a room fitted with eighteenth century cornice and salient architraves. In one of Williams' favourite details, oak panels are set in against the reveals of the opening and form, together with the twin doors and the header above, a space of its own: you are literally in the opening, in a kind of aedicular space. On either side, a new stone skirting matching the new floor is set flush with the plaster. At the junction between wall and the new linings, the plaster is cut back up to dado height and stopped with a recessed steel angle (dados were removed to simplify the wall planes). As Williams points out, the detail provides not only gravitas and weight to the doorway but also acts as an abstraction of the dado and a reminder of the original datum within the room—an abstraction of the dado that now requires us to "join up the dots in order to visually reinstate the horizontal". The room itself has generous proportions, it has been kept empty, and it is painted white. The overall effect is very quiet, pushing architecture (as said of the white reliefs of Nicholson) to the edge of extinction: it is a simple entreaty to come in and just be.

Like the Compton Verney Art Gallery, the more recent Belgrade Theatre in Coventry is an extension to a listed building, in this case a 1950s miniature version of the Royal Festival Hall in London. The composition is an assembly of simple interlocking volumes, not unlike a sculpture by Ben Nicholson sometimes used by the architects to explain the project. Hundreds of sketches and tens of models testify to subtle adjustments in their relationships, sometimes bringing them closer together, sometimes keeping them apart, until they seem no longer gratuitous but necessary. Only then will they obtain, in Stanton's words, "some kind of life and energy". The architects often talk about form as if it were an animate, active substance. In a literal sense, it is the subject of an effort, it *works*. This is a characteristic of plastic form, namely that long after it has been made solid and permanent, it appears to retain its plasticity, its capacity to be shaped, molded, modelled and sculpted, and, in turn, to give shape and meaning to human experience.

This play with forms is a first step in the progressive articulation of the building block—what Moholy-Nagy described as "the basic departure of all creative work". Then comes the division of surfaces into three-dimensional plates which together form a kind of jigsaw. The ostensible aim of this articulation is to break the scale of the building into smaller elements, thus enabling a person to better engage with it. Stanton likens these plates to a Cubist device designed "to take you round, to take you over and to take you through", reminding him of a picture of the Greek island of Delos. In this island, once a major sanctuary in antiquity, the walls, the columns, the stoas and the atria now lying in ruins form together interlocking spaces that go on and on as if endlessly, describing a city that has neither form nor elevation.

Theatre is a recurrent, underlying theme in the architecture of Stanton Williams, not in the sense given to it by postmodernism and its interest in décor but as a means to a particular interpretation of space. How far you are from a painting, from the audience or, more generally, from the presence of others, how light falls on a painting, an actor, a wall or the public are fundamental questions that are asked in any project. Oskar Schlemmer, the Master of the theatre workshop at the Bauhaus, was said to experience space "not only through mere vision but with the whole body, with the sense of touch of the dancer and the actor".[7] For Moholy-Nagy, the theatre combined sound, colour, light, motion, space, form, objects and persons. It was the art of transforming a narrative into a total plastic experience, into "a precise and fully controlled organization of form and motion".[8]

A similar procedure was adopted by Stanton Williams in the house they built near Lugano. The architects recall how the client expressed his wishes in the form of a narrative: "I work in the cool of those shading pine trees there"; "I make breakfast here looking this way", etc. These vignettes were then strung together into a kind of "living diagram" across the site.[9] Then came the task of transposing the script onto a suitable stage. "Photographing, measuring, balancing on ladders, we established angles and sequences across the site." Last the living diagram was given plastic expression through the "sculptural manipulation of carefully carved space". Like in the theatre of the Bauhaus, the task was how to integrate a sequence of human movements and thoughts with the controlled elements of architecture, namely space, light and materials. Moholy-Nagy contemplated Total Stage Action, Gropius did, Total Theatre. For Stanton Williams, the particular horizon is that of Total Architecture, of an architecture in which one is totally in control of the means at one's disposal.

Hence the central importance attached to craft. For Gropius, the artist was nothing but an exalted craftsman. "Architects, sculptors, painters, he exclaimed, we must all return to crafts!"[10] Moholy-Nagy imagined the sculptor as "a passionate and meticulous artisan".[11] Hopes for a well-crafted architecture have since been dashed. The traditional craftsman has become accessory to the building process. If he is called upon at all, it will be at the very end to apply the finishes. What is more, the construction industry has not heeded the Bauhaus programme for well-crafted, machine-made building. Yet craft remains central to Stanton Williams' approach, now in effect displaced from building to the practice of architecture itself. They make no fundamental distinction between the craftsman, the engineer and the architect. Ultimately, all are involved with the making of things. The goal—one that is becoming increasingly difficult to satisfy—is to uphold a degree of intimacy between design and its objects.

Stanton Williams proceed, as Herbert Read said of Ben Nicholson, from the play of a native sensibility with the materials of their craft.[12] The wide reach of their sources and, increasingly, of their commissions notwithstanding, Stanton Williams are an English practice and most of their work to date has been built in England. They are inheritors of a once vital English strand of modernism that included Henry Moore, Barbara Hepworth, Ben Nicholson, Herbert Read and others. The bas-reliefs of Nicholson in particular remind me of their work: the carving with hammer and chisel in fine natural materials like walnut and mahogany, the intuitive character of their composition, the several coats of paint (usually white) then vigorously rubbed down by hand to add liveliness to the surface, the sensitivity of their shallow space to natural light, the intimate character and the poetic luminosity that, more than any other aspect, underscore their spirituality. A painting, Nicholson said, "is thought, not paint".[13]

Stanton Williams' sensibility is consistent with Clive Bell's 1914 theory of Significant Form (largely adopted by Read). Bell argued that the appreciation of art required nothing but a sense of form and colour and a knowledge of three-dimensional space.[14] He recognised three characteristics in art: the absence of representation (representation will be the mainstay of postmodernism), the absence of technical swagger (high-tech architects will indulge in it), and a form considered as an end in itself. Known in the field of aesthetics as Formalism, Bell's theory was derided by the Independent Group in the 1950s for its aloofness from everyday life. This, it may have been, but to discard it, whether Bell's or European variants, was also to reject Modernism at its most original and vital.

Moreover, much depends upon one's conception of everyday life. Stanton Williams started their office with the design of exhibitions in which experience was synonymous with aesthetic contemplation. As the scale and the range of projects increased, the skills developed in these projects were applied to new programmes. In turn, the keen sensibility to aesthetic experience became projected upon the gamut of everyday life. Other architects followed suit, the museum increasingly becoming a model for other types in architecture ranging from shops to houses. But Stanton Williams' approach remains distinctive in that, better than most, they were able to shed the ideological burden of Modernism and, thanks to their background in the design of exhibitions, they were able to recover the essential plastic basis of modern architecture, and thereby its most precious gift: its liberty and its pliability to human experience.

Fuelled by the star system, architecture has been co-opted in the last 30 years by the media and by the culture industry. It became a topic of conversation, a subject for publication and a reason for travel. It was saddled with concepts and images needing to be explained before a building could be experienced. By contrast, the value of a plastic architecture lies in its directness. It is made with less mediation and it is experienced without translation. It seeks no pretext and it makes no pretense. It presents itself as no more than what it is. No longer burdened with the ideas of its authors, it seems more open to the ideas of others. Plasticity is the necessary counterpart in the world of forms to dialogue and participation in the world of men. Plasticity, Stanton Williams agree, is good.

a   *Circa 1936*, Ben Nicholson.
b   Aerial view: Delos, Cyclades Islands, Greece.
c   Edgar J Kaufmann Office, Frank Lloyd Wright, 1935.
d   *Lightplay: Black–White–Grey*, László Moholy-Nagy, 1930.
e   Museo di Castelvecchio, Carlo Scarpa, Verona, Italy, 1964.

1   van Doesburg, Theo, "Towards a plastic architecture", 1924, in Ulrich Conrads, *Programs and Manifestoes on 20th-Century Architecture*, Cambridge MA: MIT Press, 1970.
2   Stokes, Adrian, "Carving, Modelling and Agostino", in *Stones of Rimini*, London: Faber & Faber, 1934.
3   Button, Virginia, *Ben Nicholson*, London: Tate Publishing, 2007.
4   Quotes by the architects are from interviews carried out between April and June 2009, unless stated otherwise.
5   Moholy-Nagy, Laszlo, *The New Vision*, 1928.
6   Sylvester, David, letter to the Arts Council, 30 May 1984, Paul Williams archive.
7   Gropius, Walter, in *The Theatre of the Bauhaus*, Walter Gropius and Arthur S Wensinger, eds., Middletown, CN: Wesleyan University Press, 1961.
8   Gropius, *The Theatre of the Bauhaus*.
9   Williams, Stanton, "Stanton Williams in Ticino", in *Architecture Today*, no. 146, March 2004.
10 Gropius, Walter, "Programme of the Staatliches Bauhaus in Weimar", 1919, in Conrads, *Programs and Manifestoes on 20th-Century Architecture*.
11 Moholy-Nagy, *The New Vision*.
12 Read, Herbert, *Ben Nicholson: paintings, reliefs, drawings*, London: Lund Humphries, 1948.
13 Nicholson, Ben, "Notes on 'abstract' art", in Herbert, *Ben Nicholson: paintings, reliefs, drawings*.
14 Bell, Clive, *Art*, New York: Frederick A Stokes, 1914.

CONVERSATION

Alan Stanton and Paul Williams in Conversation
David Taylor

DT How would you characterise your approach to architecture? Is there a Stanton Williams ethos—and if so, did you start out with one in mind?

PW You could say that Alan and I have spent the last 23 years deliberately deflecting this question. But quite honestly, prior to agreeing to produce this book, we've never felt the need to characterise or define our approach to architecture. Our view has always been that it is the work that's important and any reflections on our work are best done by others.

Perhaps we've also been wary of formalising the position of the studio within an architectural framework or language that might typecast us in some way. Anyway, too much theory surely stultifies creativity and one's intuitive response to problem solving. We have always learnt through doing, and the practice continues to work that way.

And, of course, there is a strong Stanton Williams ethos, that has strengthened as the practice has grown, but I don't remember either Alan or I articulating our values that clearly when we set up in 1985. We enjoyed working together and had a respect for each other's work, but beyond that our primary focus was to secure interesting and challenging projects. Perhaps on a subliminal level there was a sense that collectively we might become more than the sum of our parts, but it was not something we ever discussed.

DT Was there a shared language, evident from the beginning of the partnership?

PW The development of a shared architectural language began most probably with the Miyake shops, which we conceived as carved solids or what we would call "sculpted interiors"—as opposed to an assembly of components. From the beginning, we saw the details as a very important element in our work, because they have the power to reinforce our design concepts—articulating how forms and spaces interlock, for example, emphasising the way that materials engage, pass beneath or behind each other, and also that important space between materials, created by the negative detail or the expressed joint that can be so provocative. I suppose we have always had a fundamental belief that everybody's experience of their surroundings is affected by these details, whether on a conscious or subliminal level.

With the Miyake shops we were concerned about making the activity of shopping a sensuous experience, introducing natural daylight wherever possible, carefully selecting materials, contrasting textures, and manipulating the internal volumes in order to heighten the drama and the experience for people as they moved through the spaces. That idea of the sheer enjoyment of movement through a sequence of beautifully lit interior spaces drew very much on our exhibition design experience.

DT And externally?

PW Externally, our architectural expression or language is less easy to define. For the obvious reason that each project is unique and is a response to the complexity of its surroundings. In our view, exteriors by their nature have to respond to the grain of the site; they have to be part of the landscape or contribute to the public realm, as well as expressing their own identity, and for that reason, we've never selected a ready-made palette of materials to work with. Our approach has always been born out of a desire to respond to the particularity of place, and therefore, we've never considered the idea of developing a Stanton Williams style, or adopting a formulaic approach to our architecture.

We have however, always considered working from inside to outside as a strength, in the belief that the external form should be an expression of the internal dynamics. But as is often the case, the internal spatial requirements of a brief can be at odds with the external form limited by site constraints. The resolution of the two demands is, of course, what we see as the real architectural challenge.

AS When we started out in the 1980s, we both had an enthusiasm for art. We were interested in the way artists such as Ben Nicholson dealt with materials, how they give potency to them and how space and light are explored in paintings and sculpture. Often artists are at the forefront of the exploration of these things and so inevitably we were inspired by them.

Green Quoit,
Ben Nicholson, 1967.

Herculaneum,
Campania, Italy.

In addition, we both had experience of working directly with artists and with art exhibitions and this made a significant contribution to our approach. Paul had been designing gallery and exhibition spaces and I'd been working with artists in America and France and had begun to do some exhibitions. The aesthetics of the gallery space—light, materials, scale, movement of people—became a language that we were able to extend into architectural projects. The shops that we designed for Issey Miyake took these ideas further and then larger scale building projects built on that. This has, I think, produced an architecture that is perhaps not easy to typify. Our buildings are site-specific and subtle. If you go into one of our buildings you can see what we're trying to do and you can understand it because all the layers of our work are there in the project. In a sense, you have to be there to appreciate it. Which for us, is just as it should be.

David, you brought up the question of external architectural expression—the 'object quality' of a building, if you like. The challenge for us has been similar to the problem faced by the Cubist painters, who used faceted forms and interlocking spaces that seemed to grow outwards from the centre of the painting. How to end them? Where to define the picture frame? As the scale of our projects has grown, we have come to think of the exterior as another 'interior', as it were, so that the space between buildings defines the external architecture. One could perhaps compare this to sculptors such as Moore or Calder whose works contain internal spaces but also reach out to capture large-scale spaces around them. In architecture, the Japanese house has always inspired us with its permeable spaces and strong connection between inside and out. Of course, there is a difference in scale as you move outwards—how to make the human presence felt becomes more difficult—but this way of seeing spaces nesting and interlocking, one with the other, has given us a way of taking on larger-scale projects.

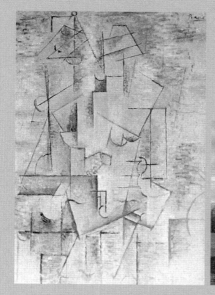

Fille et Soldat,
Pablo Picasso, 1911.

Large Two Forms,
Henry Moore, 1966.

DT Paul, you mentioned 'style' just now. That's not a notion you enjoy or approve of, is it?

PW No, the word "style" has too many connotations. Style implies a distinct manner of expression; fixed, attached to a certain look, possibly—which is not what we are about. We would like our work to be timeless, but know that's unachievable. Nevertheless, we do try not to be fashionable or influenced by trends. We have no formula; nor have we ever felt that we belong to one 'school', which would be too limiting. The culture we live in is far too rich and complex to be limited by one prescribed philosophy. I would however, like to think, that the design process in the studio is driven by an intellectual rigour that is informed by intuition as well as common sense.

We are quite relaxed about discussing the notion of 'what feels right', or how something is perceived, in terms of balance, composition, weight and so on. But ultimately we are always looking for resolution. Resolution in the sense of wholeness, where everything has been considered, and we have achieved mental clarity as well as visual clarity.

This does not discount flexibility, and the need to create spaces that do not limit or inhibit change—spaces that "allow life latitude", to quote Tadao Ando. For example, with our design for Central Saint Martins College of Art and Design's new building at King's Cross, the interior spaces will be able to evolve, and respond to changing teaching and learning environments, but importantly, within an organising architectural framework.

Covered Internal Street,
Central Saint Martins College,
King's Cross, London.

DT Taking this opportunity to reflect on your careers and portfolio thus far, are there projects missing in your 'oeuvre' that you would like to take on in the future?

AS Well, of course, the 'next project' is always going to be the special one! We are still ambitious for new challenges and I think that there are great opportunities and discoveries to be made in the future, along the course that we have set out for ourselves. This applies to both ends of the scale. We have some significant projects both in the UK and in Europe (currently the Berlin Museum and the Padua Botanic Gardens buildings) and we want to develop our work further at a city scale with important urban projects and public realm spaces; we are very interested in the way that our approach can be applied to architecture and landscape which we have explored in recent projects such as Königswinter and some of the private houses we have been designing. And, at the other end of the scale, we still like working on small projects and it would be good to design more furniture. Like Arne Jacobsen we would love to be commissioned to design a complete building from the architecture to the tableware!

Mere Farm, Wiltshire.

Padua Botanic Gardens, Italy.

DT How about in terms of the aesthetic, the materials or the palette you use? Are you seeking to be more colourful in your designs, for example?

PW No. We could have used more colour in the past and might in the future, but then we are always looking for a reason, always asking the question: why colour for its own sake? Colours are very difficult; they can often be too influential and even overwhelm a space. We still prefer to work with the more subtle colours and textures of natural materials where possible and bring them to life with natural daylight. Materials that express age and history, that become richer with the traces of wear and tear, "allow our vision to penetrate their surfaces", as Juhani Pallasmaa would say. It's those visual and tactile qualities that appeal to the senses and make the difference to how we experience things.

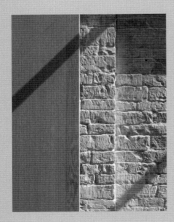

Detail, Compton Verney Art Gallery, Warwickshire.

DT And how we experience things can very often be traced back to our own personal backgrounds. Could I ask about yours? Alan first—were there key influences that have contributed to your development in design terms?

AS When I started out, coming from the provinces to London and studying at the Architectural Association it was a complete revelation to me. There was freedom, and new ideas were buzzing around. It was my kind of world—ideas, making things. I realised you could learn, and run your life by doing projects. There was a fundamental questioning of everything at the AA. By the time I left, we were all architects who were trying *not* to be architects, and trying *not* to do buildings, but covering the same territory. I think that is something that's stayed with me. I'm certainly very much an architect, but part of me doesn't like being an architect. Le Corbusier once said: "I detest talking about architecture." It's about avoiding the formulaic and conventional. Similarly, I think that's what's interesting about our practice. Both Paul and I have come from backgrounds where we learnt to question everything, and questioning conventional architectural practice means that we try and dig deeper into things. That's still the challenge and the interest, and I think that's what the AA was about for me.

DT How did you manage to develop that approach and your interests when you left the AA?

AS I realised that I needed more input and experience and also the space to experiment and build things. So, after working for Norman Foster for a year, I won a fellowship to study at the University of California in Los Angeles, where I did a Masters degree in Urban Design. In California, I was involved in setting up a company called Chrysalis with Mike Davies, Chris Dawson and a group of Los Angeles artists designing film sets, air structures, and large volume tents. We were keen to make things and even had our own workshop. We designed and built a mirrored dome for the Osaka World Expo. Then Richard Rogers asked Mike, Chris and me to come to Paris, where he and Renzo Piano had just won the Pompidou Centre competition.

Experiments in Art & Technology's Pepsi Pavilion, Expo '70, Osaka, Japan.

Reflective mylar dome prototype, Los Angeles, USA.

DT Working on the Pompidou must have been a very rich learning experience for you. What were the key lessons you gleaned from working on such an illustrious, world-famous project? What did you learn from the project team and from the personalities who would go on to be so influential to so many other designers?

AS It was a fascinating period for me, and one in which I learnt many of the skills needed to build a large project. Initially we were a very small group of architects taking the competition concept forward and developing it. I spent a lot of time with Richard Rogers. What was impressive was his generosity and sense of vision. Seeing someone operate in that visionary way was really inspiring. He encouraged me to help develop the spirit of the Pompidou building—it was how I learnt that a building project must have integrity—a soul. From Renzo Piano I learnt that a tiny, beautiful technical detail can grow into a fully-fledged building. From Peter Rice (the engineer) I learnt the art of oblique thinking. He would, in a sense, make problems for himself by turning convention upside down—I'd see him do it. He said that without interesting problems, we have no interesting solutions; we don't have anything to engage us or challenge us. I spent seven years working on the Pompidou Centre and in the last two years I worked on the interiors—the museum and gallery spaces. Ultimately, though, I found that part of the project unsatisfactory.

Gallery space, Centre Georges Pompidou, Paris, France, 1977.

DT In what way?

AS I didn't have the right degree of control of the spaces. We had put all our energy into the overall idea of the building, which was a significant, strong idea, and in spite of it being conceived as a 'flexible' framework, it did constrain what you could or couldn't do with the interior spaces which were, in effect, the end result of a 'systems' approach to design. And so, after that experience, I concluded that one should start at the other end of the design process, from the spaces themselves. It also seemed logical that you start small and then you gradually build up in scale. After the completion of the Pompidou Centre, I then started my own practice and worked on a series of projects where I began to explore some of these ideas: exhibitions, furniture systems, a design for the Durham Oriental Museum and then the La Villette Museum just before Paul and I got together.

DT Paul, could we turn now to your own background? This idea of building up in scale most probably reflects your own development, especially since before becoming a qualified architect you were more involved in art and design projects. How did that come about, and what were your own key influences?

PW I went into the sixth form at school with every intention of going on to study architecture, but I had a late change of heart and decided to apply to an arts foundation course instead. So I started at Birmingham College of Art in 1968, which for me at the time, having had a formal grammar school education, was a wonderfully liberal and liberating environment to find myself in. It's where I first encountered the world of avant-garde experimental art, the work of artists like Moholy-Nagy and his kinetic sculptures and abstract films, the Suprematist paintings of Malevich and Constructivism, Itten's colour theories and the psychological effect colour has on us, and the ideas of people like John Cage and Buckminster Fuller at Black Mountain College in America. As students then we were trying to capture the spirit of Cage's teachings and create a sort of experiential, non-centred art form, which is somewhat ironic since subsequently I have been for most of my adult life immersed in an arts and museum culture to which Cage was so opposed. It was also during that period that I was taught by Benno Zehnder, a Bauhaus influenced Swiss artist/designer who became my first significant mentor. He supported a more experimental, non-specialist design path, challenging the fundamentals of everything, and in doing so made me look at, and engage with, the world around me with a much more critical eye. I'd pick up a pencil and he'd immediately ask, "Why have you chosen that specific pencil? Have you considered its lead weight?" Why that paper, the texture, the colour, the size, and so on. He offered a critique of everything, and in so doing he challenged the way I thought. At times I can remember the process being extremely unsettling, but the questioning has stayed with me, and most probably informs much of my decision-making now.

DT What period are we talking about here?

PW This was the late 1960s, early 70s. Most probably, the first time I really engaged intellectually and emotionally with design and architecture, though, was during my postgraduate year in Birmingham. I spent a year studying a 'cube', analysing both inside and outside space, constructing large- and small-scale models, working with light, shadow and colour, and I even produced a short animated film. I was obsessed at the time with the notion of understanding, and even feeling, dimensions in space. At one point, I chose a large empty room in the college and spent hours in there, without a tape measure, trying to gauge distances, comprehend the space and its proportions. And at the same time, trying to document how the changing natural daylight altered the room's spatial qualities; its mood, its colour, and my own experience of being in it. Mind you, at the time, I had no real idea in which direction these studies were taking me. It was only when I discovered the work of Italian architect Carlo Scarpa, published in Michael Brawne's book *The New Museum: Architecture and Display* that I could see a path opening up. It was most probably those few images of Scarpa's work that seemed to offer so much potential, and the fact that I had a passion for art which led me initially into exhibition design.

DT Your next significant step in exhibition design and in terms of forging your interests was the Victoria and Albert Museum, I believe. What made you choose that institution?

PW I saw the V&A as offering the most opportunity at the time, they had a diverse exhibitions programme, and were commissioning large-scale installations—funding for exhibitions was that much greater in the 1970s and 80s. It was where I was first introduced to the 'art world'—one that was actually very supportive of design, and which, of course, for me at that time, a recently graduated student, was an extremely empowering environment to work in. Roy Strong, the director, allowed me the freedom to experiment and develop my ideas, and gave me the opportunity to design a number of wonderful exhibitions. So I was fortunate enough to be building structures and creating different types of spaces from day one. After five years at the V&A, I set up my own practice in Spitalfields, East London, in 1980, working predominantly on art exhibitions, designing installations not only in London but in some of the great museums and galleries around the world, including the Metropolitan, New York; Getty, Los Angeles; Castello Sforzesco in Milan; and the Palazzo Vecchio in Florence. It was an endless stream of deadlines, but a very creative period for me, and of course I was also meeting and working with some wonderful artists and curators. David Sylvester, the irrepressible art critic and curator who was a regular visitor during Hayward Gallery installations, always said that exhibition design was a magical and elusive act best compared to the act of conducting an orchestra—except that conductors receive rather more attention. Mind you, I think that equally applies to architecture.

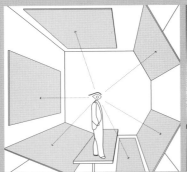

DT I'm interested in how your worlds collided, both of you. How did you meet?

PW We had been selected to work on the same project—*Paint and Painting* at the Tate. Prior to that we had never met.

DT This was an exhibition?

AS Yes, I was designing two temporary pavilions on the lawns in front of the Tate and Paul was designing an installation in the Duveen Galleries. We met and worked alongside each other, but then I won a competition in Paris with Mike Dowd for a major exhibition space at the new La Villette Museum. It was possibly 18 months later when I returned from Paris that we next met. Paul was being offered a number of interesting projects and initially suggested to me that it would be great if we could work together on one of them. So our first joint project was completed in 1984 at the V&A Boilerhouse Gallery in South Kensington, the Coca Cola Exhibition commissioned by Stephen Bayley.

Coca-Cola (exhibition), Boiler House Gallery, V&A Museum, London, 1986.

DT And what was it that you saw as working between you?

PW That's difficult to say. Alan had the experience of working on the Pompidou Centre and La Villette, whereas my work drew its inspiration from the work of Scarpa and Kahn. At first glance, two different backgrounds and approaches to architecture, but on a fundamental level, we shared the same values, similar sensibilities and had a mutual respect that allowed us to challenge and question each other as we began to explore new territory.

DT Do you see yourselves as opposites combining to produce something greater than the sum of its parts, as it were?

PW No, definitely not opposites, more that we complemented each other. I wanted the challenge of larger building projects and Alan was looking for more focused work. At the time, I was being asked if I would consider more architectural work and could see the potential of this work on the horizon. So it was ideal for me to form a partnership with Alan, because I wasn't, at that stage, a registered architect. Our first competition entry, which we won, was to design a new exhibition gallery on the RIBA's Portland Place sculpture court. We then entered the competition for the extension to the National Portrait Gallery and won that also. So, within three months of forming our partnership we had secured two major building projects. The fact that neither got built due to lack of funding was very disappointing, but clearly the sum of the parts, as you say, was working. Having said that, it was quite a while before we managed to complete our first building, a small artist's studio in South London.

RIBA Architecture Centre and
Sculpture Court gallery, Portland
Place, London.

Artist's Studio, London.

AS We both came from different directions and found ourselves in a similar place. Paul wanted to expand the architectural scale, and I had been working on large-scale things, which was exciting, but I felt that I wanted to work on projects where I could be more 'hands on'. I had a lot of respect for what Paul was doing and saw that he had total control over an exhibition space—the lighting, the materials, the graphics—everything was controlled, and that was the direction I wanted to move in. So, it seemed to me that if we could put this together, our combined experience, then we'd have something really special with a tremendous range and power because of its integrity.

DT What period was this?

AS We're talking about the early 1980s. It was very hard for young architects to get projects, but with exhibitions there was an opportunity to get things built. We're not 'paper architects'—we both love the craft of making things. There's nothing like it. We both love going into factories and seeing things made, the smell of wood and metal. Paul had metal workers and joinery shops that he was using all over the city, so it was wonderful for me too. To see things being made, talking with and learning from craftsmen. I'd had that experience in my own projects but it was the immediacy of it that really appealed to me. On a building contract, you have the discussion and then six months later you might get the working drawings, and six months after that you see something being built. But with exhibitions, the turnaround time is so fast that you have a discussion, you draw it on a piece of paper and you go the next day and it's being built. It's all there, and then three months later it's gone, it's been removed, and you're on to the next show.

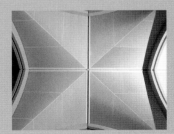

Tensile fabric ceiling, Age
of Chivalry (exhibition),
Royal Academy of Arts,
London, 1987.

DT Would you say exhibition design is a good starting point for any architect? Would you advocate it?

AS Absolutely, yes.

DT Because of the issues of scale?

AS Because it has the fundamentals of architecture—space and light and materials—and because it's a way of learning how people and objects relate to spaces.

PW And, of course, their immediacy is intoxicating. They allow you the room to experiment. Structures are erected so quickly you literally experience the enclosure being formed around you, witness the actual capturing of space, and feel the impact it has on your body, emotions even. You can't experience that with a building—the construction process is too slow.

DT The principles of exhibition design are, presumably, manifest in all your schemes?

PW I think the principles are very evident in our early work and remain embedded in the design culture of our studio. We still see exhibition design as an important part of the Stanton Williams portfolio.

DT It strikes me that the broad concepts of an *appropriate* architectural scale, craft, and materials are central to your work as a practice.

AS Yes they are. The nature of materials and the way things are made and put together is fundamental to the way that we design. Learning how things are made should be a fundamental prerequisite for any architect's training. The Bauhaus teaching programme taught students how to work in metal, glass, wood and so on. You go through all that training before you can start to design. Then you design a piece of furniture, then you design a room, then you design a house, before you work up to—or even start thinking about—anything at an urban or landscape scale. We both believe that, at a fundamental level, designing a door handle detail should not be much different to designing a whole building. And yes, I think our practice has grown in that way.

Door detail, Issey Miyake Women, London.

We start with the human form. Issey Miyake talks about the space between the body and the clothes. The clothes are like the first manifestation of something that is vaguely architectural. Beyond that, you start to have furniture and then the room itself. This was for us the exhibition space, the shops, the interiors and the buildings that we started to design together. Our confidence grew as the scale of the projects grew, and on the way we were learning to develop a common language and a way of operating.

Initially, we were concerned about growing too quickly because that intensity and that commitment had to be spread over much larger projects, so we managed the process of growing quite carefully. Occasionally, of course, larger-scale opportunities would come up and you had to make a big leap, and that was the challenge, not in terms of our ambition or confidence but in terms of maintaining the quality. What was critical was to maintain the strength and, you might say, essence of what we had achieved in our earlier projects.

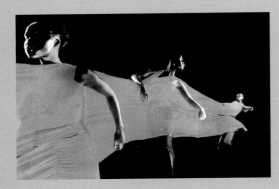

A-Poc 1999, Issey Miyake.

DT Did that 'essence' ever get away from you?

AS Well, when we won the Sloane Avenue project in competition (our first large building), we handled it well and found it to be a relatively easy transition into larger-scale work. The project was extremely successful and the essential qualities of light, space and detailing worked really well throughout that building.

Entrance and atrium,
60 Sloane Avenue, London.

Nowadays, the whole studio enjoys the challenge of working on increasingly larger-scale and more demanding projects. There seems to be a natural progression of our thinking as we move up in scale. We have been able to apply our early experience of internal spaces to the design of larger interiors such as the entrance and atrium at 4 Brindleyplace in Birmingham. However, for the exterior of that project, we had to develop a way of analysing the spaces around the building, the square and the streets, so that the architecture could then be formed within those external spaces.

Exterior and colonnade,
4 Brindleyplace,
Birmingham.

This approach was then further developed on the Bristol department store project and the Belgrade Theatre. We also discovered that we were looking at people moving in a different way in a much larger space, with a far grander scale so we then started applying some of these ideas to new public spaces such as Tower Hill and Sloane Square. We had to understand the way people use and move through open spaces and the architecture was formed around that. This, of course, related all the way back down the chain of our ideas, back to the way people move through exhibition spaces

DT How do you work as a pair and as a studio? And has that altered much over the years as you have grown and taken on larger projects?

PW In the early days we worked very closely together but less so now because as you suggest, our projects are that much more complex. But in those first years, an understanding between us developed that has evolved into a kind of Esperanto. In design sessions now, a line drawn or a word spoken is often enough to know where each other's thoughts are coming from. But we're no longer joined at the hip. Now the design mix in the studio is rich in other ways. The studio has grown in size, and we have a number of really talented designers working with us, especially our co-directors—Peter Murray, Patrick Richard and Gavin Henderson. They are great guys who have been working with us for many years and are now influential players who, each in their own way, add to the chemistry. Patrick, Gavin and Peter have added greatly to the design development of the practice as well as in reinvigorating the core characteristics of our work. And Peter has almost single-handedly overseen our transition from a small team of 15 in east London to our present studio of over 50 people.

Paul Williams, Patrick Richard,
Alan Stanton, Peter Murray
and Gavin Henderson.

AS In the studio these days it is a form of creative teamwork with Patrick, Gavin, Peter and others contributing to the 'language' and pushing it forward into new areas. We have always been passionate about hand sketches and making models, sometimes even at a very large scale, and see them as essential design tools. This has become an integral part of our studio culture. Models allow us to explore carving, assembling, forming, and folding. Working with cardboard, chunks of stone, wood, steel and glass—checking, measuring, explaining and working with clients and engineers—plotting spaces and details. This three-dimensional way of working is, for us, the best way to develop and understand subtle and complex spaces and forms. It is, if you like, a way of 'being there' and feeling what it's like, just another tool to help us get at the essence of the thing.

PW Yes, using models as a design tool is central to helping us mentally inhabit the spaces we are creating, but also they offer 3-D representations of designs that everyone can understand and engage with, especially clients. Models promote dialogue, and dialogue with the client is the fundamental design tool in the initial stages of a project, when the brief can be properly interrogated, and goals and aspirations explored.

DT Do you think that as a practice you have a unique voice, ethos or oeuvre?

PW At one level, everyone is unique, but we don't see the pursuit of the unique and the novel as the basis for design. I would like to think that our work is distinguished by our continued attention to detail and craft, and aspiring to architecture that is rooted in sensory experience—the way people experience place.

DT You have, of course, been involved with many notable projects on sensitive historic sites. Are you in fact *more* comfortable working with heritage than with new build?

PW We are comfortable working with heritage, but not more comfortable. Renzo Piano said he's at his most creative and happiest when he's most restricted, and feels totally at ease when he understands the parameters. I have to say, I support that view. We've undertaken a number of projects working within listed historic buildings such as Compton Verney and Whitby Abbey that have required intricate, contemporary interventions that take time to both research and execute, and always have complex planning issues to address. With all these projects, the historic grain must be understood and respected, so that when a new intervention—a new layer—is inserted, the juxtaposition of old and new will heighten the qualities of each constituent part and create something that is significantly better as a whole. These buildings can often be part of a city, part of a history, but no longer playing any role or no longer sustainable—needing to be reborn with a new purpose. It's this rebirth that we find so fascinating.

AS Over the years I think that we have made an important contribution to changing people's attitudes to historic sites and buildings in this country. It used to be that new and old did not mix—they were kept well apart. This was due perhaps not only to conservation organisations but also to modernists who believed that modern buildings had to be pure and a 'totality'. 20 years ago it was really difficult—you were either a restoration architect or you were a modern architect and the two were not in sight of each other. We challenged that, and always felt that the new could make an important contribution to the old and, of course, *vice versa*—that it was the natural way of things. Just look at rich historical sites and see the layers of changes and additions that have been made over the centuries. We were inspired by contemporary Italian designers such as Scarpa, Canali and Veneziana, who had been working with new and old in Europe for years. So our work at Compton Verney and Whitby Abbey, I would say, helped shift the orthodox view of conservation in this country. People could see that the thoughtful and creative interweaving of historic and contemporary elements could really work and could even produce something very special.

DT I want to shift to the other extreme and ask you about how you approach the notion of the icon or object building. I think much of the propensity for the object quality of building can be attributed to ego—can't it? And you strike me as being anti-ego. You're the antithesis of icon architecture.

AS Yes, I think we are, in the contemporary media's shallow definition of the words. Why does a building have to be an object? Why does it have to be iconic? I find this thing about uniqueness and the object quality of building most difficult because it's so much of what's going on, or has been going on for the last ten to 15 years. Architects have been buying into this idea—we don't. Philip Dowson said that a building is a process, not a commodity, and one can sense that today there is a certain exhaustion with glittering, one-off buildings. To us, that suggests the idea that a calmer, more unified approach might be around the corner. Architecture can be visionary, rich, complex and subtle without spectacular forms. In a sense, we feel that a building should be at one with everything around it and within it. That is not to say at all that it's invisible, but that it has its own particular characteristics that express themselves in more subtle ways.

DT So, now that you are working on a larger scale of projects, what does that mean for your approach? And what are some of the other challenges that come with that? What are you trying to do now and in the future, as Stanton Williams?

AS Well these days much of our work is to do with cities and public spaces. We certainly enjoy the challenge of urban projects, despite the often demanding constraints and complexities. Le Corbusier was right when he said that, urban schemes are often "rational and poetic monuments set up in the midst of contingencies". The city also provides a rich context that is a source of ideas and inspiration and our experience of working on complicated, often sensitive, projects in the past now gives us ways of creatively engaging with complex urban problems, with larger-scale spaces and multiple uses.

Granary Square, Central Saint Martins College and canal-side Pavilion, King's Cross, London.

As I already mentioned, the architectural climate is perhaps changing at last and we might begin to speculate about the idea of a 'public architecture', something that is built around the way that people operate socially and together. Sigfried Giedion wrote about how, in the nineteenth century, people complained that all the dignity had gone out of ordinary life. Maybe we are now in a similar transition period. We have to ask ourselves "how do we want to live?" We must put the human being back at the centre of things again, to revitalise the city with spaces that embody key common values and that are defined by human scale, energy and warmth—to make what Pallasmaa calls "islands of authenticity". We would like to think that this means there is a strong case for an architecture that is well ordered, well proportioned and human. Something that puts the aesthetics of the city and its spaces first.

PW Things like order, proportion, rhythm, structure and the human presence are common to great architecture of any age, and in that sense I'd say that we have some of our roots in the classical tradition as well as the modern. And it is interesting that many of the great modernists—such as Le Corbusier, Kahn, and Wright, amongst others—measured themselves against those traditions. So maybe it really is time to re-emphasise that kind of continuity, rather than so-called 'originality'.

Compacted earth blades, Yemen.

We need to continue to learn from the past. Say, for example, from a building like Durham Cathedral that can trigger such strong emotions. That building exudes an energy that is almost tangible, mystifying, but at the same time spiritually uplifting. It affirms a belief that good architecture has the ability to tap into our emotions and, by engaging our senses, has the power to improve the quality of our life. That must surely be our ultimate goal.

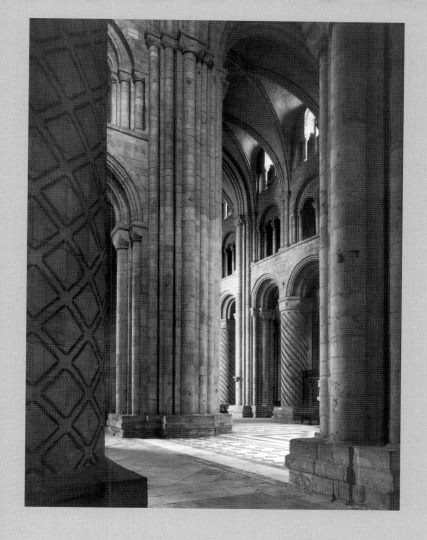

Durham Cathedral.

ISSEY
MIYAKE

Stanton Williams have worked on a number of projects for the designer Issey Miyake. They found that they had a natural sympathy for his use of textures, space and movement, and in a variety of locations, they have tried to create spaces that reflect and complement his clothes. The projects aimed to create a strong sense of presence, with restrained, sculptural spaces, dramatised by the clothes, drawing in as much natural light as possible to what were frequently awkwardly shaped and basement areas. The designs incorporate natural materials—from Italian hand-crafted marmarino (a luminous and reflective mixture of marble dust and plaster), Portland stone, to oak and maple fittings. Displays were often 'carved' into walls, with pull-out shelves to maximise space.

**Issey Miyake 'Men',
Brompton Cross, London, 1987.**

(Above) The three metre high oak entrance doors open to reveal a triple-height, vaulted space.

(Opposite) Marmarino plaster and forged steel hanger, detail.

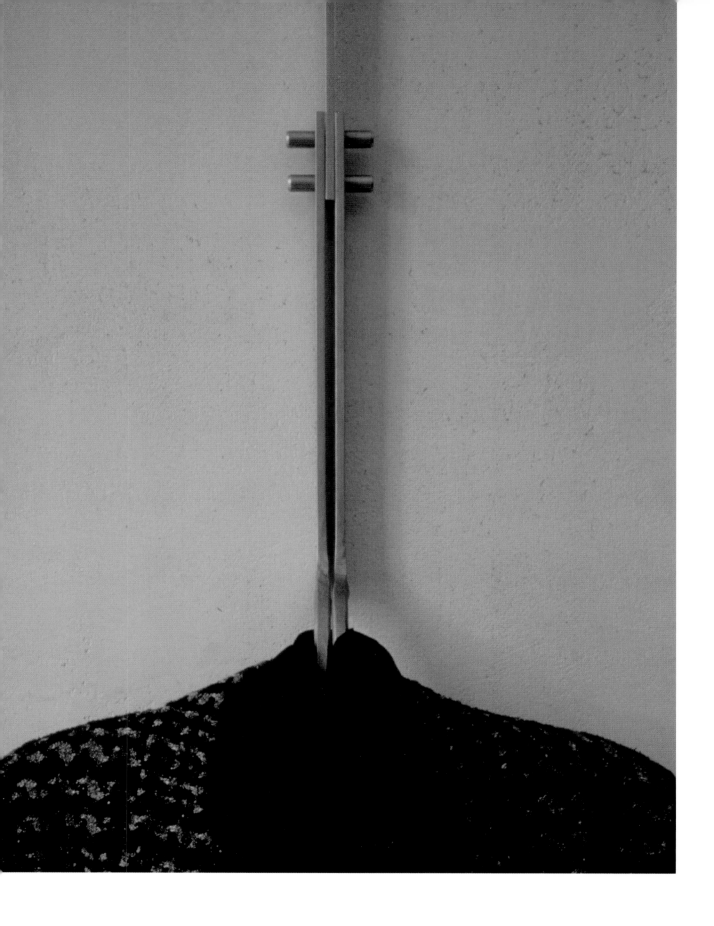

(Above left) The triple-height volume was created by the removal of most of the first floor and half of the existing ground floor. The space is up-lit from concealed fittings at the base of the vaulted ceiling. Natural daylight, entering through a newly created roof light, draws the visitor to the rear of the space.

(Above right) Early design sketch for the space.

(Opposite) A broad limestone stair leading down to the main retail area and changing rooms.

Issey Miyake 'Women',
Brompton Cross, London, 1988.

(Above) In contrast to the man's
shop (on the other side of the
road), the facade of the women's
shop is more transparent, with the
emphasis on the interior space.
The solid timber doors are replaced
by glass with timber and stainless
steel door handles signalling the
entrance threshold.

(Opposite) The triangular-shaped
ground floor space. In order to
create a generous space for a
new staircase, most of the ground
floor and back wall were removed.
Coffered ceiling, glazed roof light
and double-height etched glass
window encourage movement to
the main retail floor below. The walls
and ceiling are finished in raw pink
and white plaster with expressed
stainless steel corner beads.

(Above) A lower landing confronts
the clothes that are hung on a
single rail that extends along
the full length of the space.

(Opposite) Detail of the handrail
with a glimpse of the timber
screened changing rooms.

**Issey Miyake 'Pleats Please',
Brook Street, London, 1996.**

(Opposite) Display unit suspended over the newly created ground floor void with the sliding acrylic shelves designed to hold the Issey Miyake range of 'Pleats Please' garments.

(Above) An open stair links the two display areas and the floor void allows refracted natural light to enter and animate the lower retail area.

Issey Miyake 'Women' Conduit Street, London, 1999.

(Above) A glass and stainless steel stair leads down to the lower retail area within a newly created opening in the ground floor.

(Right) The ground floor display area with a light sculpture by Ingo Maurer. A pink pigmented marmarino plaster screen acts as a backdrop to the space and conceals generously proportioned changing rooms.

(Overleaf) Sunlight interacting with the glass and stainless steel balustrade and staircase.

Issey Miyake
London, UK

Between 1985 and 1999, Stanton Williams worked on several projects for Issey Miyake, providing the renowned Japanese designer with a series of stores which reflect and complement the texture and movement of his clothes. Each commission demonstrates an individual approach, but certain themes bring them together. The spaces simultaneously possess a strong presence whilst drawing back to allow Miyake's clothes to take centre stage. Much attention was given to the textural possibilities of quality materials, complemented by a considered approach to light (both artificial and natural). The geometries and juxtapositions of textures, balustrades and floor levels were conceived, together with lighting, to draw the eye into and through the stores, providing a framework for display and physical movement. The results seek to transcend passing fashion by instead appealing to the fundamentals of architecture.

The first commission for Miyake comprised a menswear store within a narrow Victorian property on London's Brompton Road, Knightsbridge, completed in 1987. The original floor levels were removed (with the exception of the uppermost floor), creating a heightened vertical scale that countered the narrowness of the premises. The width of the ground floor was split, one half housing a stair that led down to the basement sales area, and the other functioning as a gallery overlooking that space. Above, in the area formerly occupied by the first floor, a split semi-circular vault captured and contained the volume of the store. A glazed opening in the ceiling at the rear allowed light to permeate through to basement level, while artificial lighting was carefully concealed so that light and space would seem as one.

Movement into and through the store was central to the articulation of the space. Thus the weight of the solid oak entrance doors, flanked by glazed screens, emphasised the threshold between street and internal space. Throughout, the geometries of different elements and materials interlocked, their inter-relationships structuring the movement of the eye through space as a counterpart to the physical act of entering and moving through the store.

The prevailing palette reflected the natural fibres that then dominated Miyake's work: stone, steel and timber, used in a natural, discreetly textured state. Marmarino plaster, applied to the walls, was chosen for its depth and substance, imbuing the shop with the sense that it had been almost carved from rock. The treads of the stair were Portland stone, while a blasted steel balustrade sailed above panels of structural glass. The same steel was used for clothes hangers, fixed like picture hooks into recessed grooves such that clothes gave the impression of being located freely in space.

The men's shop was followed in 1988 by one opposite, for Miyake's women's ranges, again largely located at basement level. This time, however, the entrance was given a predominantly glazed treatment, with door handles of wood and steel. The robust marmarino wall treatment of the men's shop was replaced by softer, more feminine raw pink and white plaster finishes. Open-tread stairs led down through a full-height void to a slightly-raised plinth at one side of the showroom, the idea being that this area could be extended and used as a catwalk. The main part of the basement featured clothes hung to one side; at the other, a glazed area admitted light from a courtyard garden. Generous fitting rooms were conceived as celebrating the act of changing into and wearing Miyake's clothes.

The third Miyake commission comprised a shop in Smith Street, Chelsea, for the "Plantation" range, with offices and pied-a-terre above. Opened in 1990, the store was located in a residential street. It operated very much 'by invitation only', giving a sense of the showroom being, in fact, a domestic room. Clothes were concealed behind full-height wooden screens at the edges of the room, which was treated simply. The design, as with other Miyake commissions, included several pieces of bespoke furniture.

Six years later, Miyake commissioned a further store, this time for his "Pleats Please" range in Brook Street, Mayfair. Pleats Please, launched in 1993, comprises garments made from single sheets of polyester fabric, which are heat treated to generate permanent pleats. Form and texture thus emerge simultaneously. The artificial fabrics of the range stimulated a slightly different approach to architectural design, as did the way in which the garments are sold, rolled up like posters. To one side of the ground-floor showroom, a series of sliding acrylic trays were created, stacking above each other like an open-fronted chest of drawers and suspended over a new opening in the floor. Light entering the basement was thus filtered through constantly-changing layers of fabric and acrylic, creating a shimmering effect below.

A second shop for Pleats Please followed in 2000. And the year before had brought a commission for a further Miyake store on Conduit Street, Mayfair. Once more, the intention was to create a collage of light and texture that would complement the clothes on display. Thus, for example, a pink screen slides in front of a large opaque window, screening the fitting rooms behind, while light is filtered through a glazed stair and across a dramatic ceiling sculpture to generate dappled effects. Again, the interlocking nature of materials, planes and textures creates a series of 'lines' that draw the eye through the space, dissolving the columns that support the building's upper levels and breaking down the scale of the store.

The aim in all of these projects was to create an architecture that could function as a restrained backdrop to the clothes for sale and which would respond to Miyake's changing designs. But this backdrop was never intended to be entirely neutral, nor fixed. The shops are all formed, controlled spaces intended to draw people in and orchestrate their movements. Changing patterns of natural and artificial light add to the stores' ambience, combining with their geometries and materials to generate welcoming spaces.

A Pure Space
Stanton Williams' 1987 Commission for Issey Miyake
Irénée Scalbert

I design the space between the body and the clothes... my responsibility is only half—the rest lies with the wearer, she adds as much as I do. Issey Miyake

In 1978, Norman Foster completed a shop for the clothing chain Joseph on a prominent corner site in London. In keeping with the supermarket aesthetic then dominant, its interior was in full view of passers-by. Garments were hung without ceremony on standardised racks behind a large expanse of plate glass. Within the next ten years, all this was to change. Away from the high street, the new temples of fashion became harder to find. Often the name of the shop or even the street number alone was deemed sufficient. Almost ten years after the shop for Joseph, Foster designed another for fashion designer Kathryn Hamnett. It revealed nothing of its contents. All that could be seen from Brompton Road was a glass bridge that transported the customer through a covered way into the exotic world of fashion. The fashion shop had become a pure interior.

In 1985 Alan Stanton and Paul Williams received their first architecture commission from Issey Miyake.[1] Also on Brompton Road, the shop was completed in 1987 and existed for a mere three years.[2] It had no facade to speak of. On the outside, a pair of two-storey fabric banners, stamped with the name of Issey Miyake in a frail sans-serif typeface, did what they could to conceal a meagre Victorian house. Beneath the banners, two timber doors of a height and weight fit for a chapel, were framed with large sheets of plate glass. Solidity was not where you expected it, and the simple monumental doors did much to slow you down at the moment of entry. What lay behind was described at the time as a shrine, a tomb, a gallery, and only last as a menswear shop.[3] With the exception of one or two jackets hung high on the wall, there was nothing to see except an unusually tall and deep space. As a critic observed at the time, the mood of the space was powerful well beyond its modest scale.[4] It did more than make an impression: It was intimidating. Entering a fashion shop prompts a degree of self-consciousness (Am I suitably dressed? Have I got means?). Moreover the retail area proper was situated in the basement, and you needed confidence to move down the stairs, the more so since men's fashion shops were then a novelty.

Fashion was more exclusive, more experimental than it is today. Miyake's collections in particular were like essays in clothing whose topic was the space between cloth and skin. Even more than Mariano Fortuny's collections at the beginning of the twentieth century, they appealed to architects for whom each fashion shop was an essay in design. Before he and Williams set up their office in 1985, Stanton had practiced in Paris, where the fashion shops in and around the Place des Victoires, then mostly Japanese, made an impression. Walls had been stripped back to stone or concrete or were painted white, and furniture was made of rusty iron. Sometimes the effect was not fully intended. Maureen Doherty, a friend of Miyake and his representative for London, organised the opening party for Miyake Women designed by David Chipperfield in Sloane Street, London. Flights from Japan and Europe had been booked. The project was two or three months late, and there was at this stage not much more than a concrete shelf in the space. In a couple of days, Doherty fitted theatre lights, put six garments on the wall, spread sawdust on the floor and installed Issey Miyake at a table at the rear of the shop. Guests from *Domus* and elsewhere assumed that it was a new way of designing shops and exclaimed that it was "Incredibile! Minimalista!" Reviews were favourable. Clearly on this occasion the Emperor had no clothes, but the anecdote illustrates the freedom and the aesthetic that then prevailed at the high end of fashion.

In the 1980s, James Stirling, Norman Foster, and Richard Rogers stood in a position comparable to that which Wright, Le Corbusier, and Mies had occupied. The Neue Staatsgalerie,1984, the Hong-Kong and Shanghai Bank, 1986, and the Lloyds building, 1986, were watersheds for their designers and for architecture in Britain generally. For younger architects wishing to strike out on their own, it was a demanding period when great projects were built, old dogmas were abandoned, and no new doctrines prevailed.[5] The next generation, including designers like David Chipperfield Architects and Stanton Williams, has been sparing in its use of words and manifested itself first and foremost in its works. To the technological positivism of High-Tech, they responded with an architecture that appealed directly to the senses; to the tactile rather than the visionary, to permanence rather than flexibility. To the formalism and the historical allusions of post modernism, they responded with an appeal to the spirit and a deeper sense of history. During this period, Louis Kahn returned to the canon, and the complete works of Carlo Scarpa (which Williams had studied many years earlier) were published in 1985. Interest in traditional aspects of Japanese culture was widespread, and words of praise were common about Cistercian architecture and other buildings in which light was the principle form of ornament.

What has made Stanton Williams' approach distinctive from the start has been a deliberate, consistent emphasis on interior space. Rather than working from the outside, they design the interior and work their way out—something that became more typical as the scale of the projects in the practice increased. This approach owes much to their experience in designing art exhibitions[6] in which objects, space, light, and movement matter equally. Attention is concentrated not on the object alone but on the space and the people in that space, and it is on this basis that they have developed their elusive language. By contrast with recent iconic architecture, their work does not prioritize formal identity. It makes up for it with a strong spatial character, and it is this character that contributes over the long term to the identity of its occupants. The approach is clearly indebted to the Modern tradition, but it differs from it in that space instead of the plan is the generator. Stanton Williams were recommended to Maureen Doherty by Richard Rogers.[7] With the site on Brompton Road already bought and the project under way, Stanton Williams met Miyake in Paris during a fashion show. Through the lunch that followed, there was little opportunity to discuss the brief. In response to the architects' questions, Miyake picked up a jacket that lay by his side and said: "Do you feel this? If you understand the quality of this, that's what I want. That's the brief for the shop." And so it was about tactile quality and sensuality.

Doherty did not want a conventional retail space prettified with colours and bright lights. She dreamt of a space where clothes would be merely incidental and where anything could be sold. She was of course involved in fashion, but she was first and foremost an artist. Like Miyake with clothes, like Stanton and Williams with architecture, she intuitively looked for a quality that was fundamental to the setting of a shop. She wanted a "good space" that existed in the moment, where staff could iron clothes before hanging them on the wall. A shopkeeper's responsibility, she argues, is to the customer as much as it is to the owner. A shop is social as well as commercial. Customers, she claims, seldom know what they want and seek the reassurance offered by labels. A good shopkeeper takes away the decision from the customer—like a French butcher who announces that he has something special for you, disappears at the back of the shop and returns triumphant with a choice cut (Doherty then lived in Paris). Goods therefore need not be on display. This is what happened in the Miyake shop, where clothes were hung in the basement. Doherty brought pages ripped from magazines—*The Economist*, style and photography magazines—to her meetings with the architects, and she would leave them behind. She was the agent as well as a friend of Miyake, and her job was to bring the architects as close to him as possible. Thus the brief came to Stanton Williams on the form of suggestions rather than instructions. There was talk of fire ("Miyake loves fire and water"), and a fireplace was envisaged at the far end of the shop (the fire officer put an end to this). Photographs brought to the table included mud huts and primitive things carved or assembled in a child-like way. Doherty talked about the spaces of the Musée de Cluny in Paris, about the weight and the presence of stone. This prompted the choice of marmorino, a mix of marble dust and plaster for the floors and walls. "We would have liked", the architects recall, "to have carved the space out of stone."

The premises leased for the shop were small and naturally inspired a desire to make them more spacious. Except for the third floor, the building was gutted, removed of what was most valuable commercially. With a turnover of £100 million and 300 employees, Miyake already had a large business, but neither he nor Doherty was retail-minded. And so you entered through the big timber doors, and before, above, and below you was only space. At 3.7 metres, this space was narrow, at 12 metres, it was relatively shallow, but at nine metres, it was unusually high. Hence the eye was drawn upward to the brightly illuminated vault, forward to a new skylight casting brightness into the basement, and downwards onto the relatively shallow stairs. The plan was split down its length into two halves, one half leading via a stairway that was like a see-through piece of sculpture to a small art gallery above the vault (intended but never realised), and the other going down to the retail floor. Also split were the doors that you "broke open" on entry. Even the vault was split down its length, tacitly to acknowledge that it was not structural.

The architects describe the shop interior as a box and compare its role to the stage proscenium in a theatre. A shop gives one some of a director's control over space, perspective, light, colour, clothes, and, in some limited way, action and movement. Hence the designers' use of models—effectively miniature theatres—as a means of projecting themselves into a space. A sectional model was made for the Miyake shop, its purpose being to "get your head into it". In this way, when a project does get built and one walks into it, the likelihood is that it will feel right.

The architects hesitated over the design of the vault. Postmodern arches were much in evidence, and the architects were worried about it being perceived as a postmodern or classical device. Certainly it was indebted to the Kimbell Art Museum (Williams had long been an admirer of Kahn), though the vault at Miyake was semicircular rather than elliptical. Also the way in which the soffit was brought down below the spring of the arch and then sharply trimmed where it intersects with the ceiling at the rear, all this—the sharpness, the concision, the volumetric abstraction—brought to mind the entrance space of the Clore Gallery at the Tate then recently completed by James Stirling. So did the monumental cornices (concealing light fittings) that ran along the impost line of the vault. But the vault did the right thing with the space: It contained it, it reflected light down, and helped return the eye downwards to the retail floor. To override one's reservations about form, style, or fashion so long as it feels right, so long as it works best, is consistent with the belief that architecture is justified only by the experience it accommodates.

The range of materials was intentionally restricted as in Luis Barragán's work (admired by the architects) without the colours. Stone, steel, and timber were used in their natural state and were occasionally finished to be more according to their nature: Portland stone for the treads of the main stairs, marmorino (it has more depth and substance than plaster), bright steel for the balustrade and hangers (it is less shiny than stainless steel), English oak (less patterned than American oak). All were materials with less pattern and more texture than are the norm in interiors. The overall effect was understated, more so than in David Chipperfield's earlier shop for Issey Miyake on Sloane Street, where the large marble panel facing the entrance recalled the modern classicism of Loos, Terragni, and others.

Reserve did not preclude expression. Grooves everywhere delineated and articulated the edges of things. The steel flats of balusters reached down from the handrail (not all the way to the ground, the glass on either side being structural) and punctuated its length. Cloth hangers were fixed like picture rods into a recessed cyma. They consisted of steel flats, extended by two additional flats that bent forward into the space and reached outward to form the two shoulders of the hanger. In this way, clothes fell freely in space and cast a shadow on the wall. Hanger, baluster, tread, wall panel: each element was complete in itself, and all carefully interlocked with their neighbours.

The architecture that emerged in London in the 1980s was neither white nor grey, as it had been in America. It was, so to speak, beige. Materials conveyed something of their origins in nature, but they showed little expression in themselves. They were not left in a raw state to show the mark of the saw, of the trowel or the foundry, as they had been by the Brutalists. Nor were they polished in an imitation of perfection and an invitation to touch. Neither dark in colour nor (patterned like tropical woods or expensive marbles, they instead offered the essence of discretion. The aim was not to create a minimal, more abstract architecture. Rather, the effect of all this restraint was to make space, the space between the materials and the self, seemingly palpable. It became a means of enhancing space and human presence, just as a sudden silence makes a conversation or a melody clearly audible.

In a recent lecture, Williams recalled Barragán's observation that the concepts of serenity and silence, of intimacy and amazement, had disappeared from publications on architecture.[8] Spaces designed by the practice often have these qualities. They are contemplative, and to appreciate them requires time in them. At a certain level, they reflect the temperamental preferences of their designers. They also reflect the close association in the modern mind between space and silence. In the Plan Voisin, Le Corbusier had called forth a spectacle of grandeur and serenity, or cars hurtling like meteors into the night. For Louis Kahn, silence was an essence that preceded architecture, about to be made real by the touch of light. These metaphysics of modern space have yet to be articulated.

In such spaces, as in churches hushed by religious customs or in galleries quieted by the canons of artistic experience, sound seems hemmed in. The loss in conversation and liveliness is compensated by an increased awareness of visions and by the greater care attached to light, its colour, focus, and intensity. In the Miyake shop, unlike in so many shops that sparkle with low-voltage lights, the architects wanted to show light without showing the light fittings. These were concealed above cornices or buried within the depths of soffits so that light seemed at one with space. At the time of completion, the shop was cited as evidence that the "pure flame" of Modernism had been passed to a new generation.[9] It inherited from High-Tech and the Bauhaus (an early defining influence on Williams), a belief in "good design", in the value of problem-solving, fitness for purpose and appropriateness. But it had evolved in one significant respect. Space no longer "flowed" as it did for Modernists. It was captured and contained, and it became infused with a characteristic stillness that gave satisfaction, peace of mind, and pleasure. You could now feel the space when you moved into it, as you do when entering water.

The point of this design, however, was not its modernity. For Miyake no less than for Stanton Williams, design is about the space between body and material. Like Miyake's Permanente collection that was stocked in the shop, it is about slowing things down, about making things that do not date. Permanente consists in re-workings of Miyake's best designs. It aims to reach beyond the seasonal ("this was the summer of 87") or even a particular decade ("this was very 80s"). For Stanton and Williams, this approach was a retort to the fleeting designs of postmodernism. It remains today a possible answer to the insistent demands made by clients for iconic buildings and celebrity. The worse thing about the 1980s, Miyake has said, is that designers became stars. Design is not an extension of one's ego: it is teamwork. It employs many people, and it carries responsibility.[10] Stanton and Williams understand this. For the last 20 years, they have quietly carved a path that makes no reference to objects, styles, or concepts, and this protects them from the crisis now facing the architectural imagination, caught between a seemingly insatiable appetite for difference and a desire for more lasting significance.

This essay was first published in the Fall/Winter 2008–2009 edition of the *Harvard Design Magazine*.

1   This article is based upon interviews in May 2008 with Alan Stanton, Paul Williams, and Maureen Doherty.
2   In 1990, Stanton Williams designed a new shop for Issey Miyake across the road at no. 270. It still exists, and several more were built for the company in the years that followed. The original shop was refurbished for Betty Jackson. The vault and a few steel fittings were retained but little of the original design remains.
3   Davies, Colin, "A Fetish for Fashion", in *Designers' Journal*, November 1987.
4   Amery, Colin, *Chipperfield, Mather, Parry, Stanton & Williams: Four London Architects, 1985–88,* London and Cambridge: 9H Gallery and MIT Press, 1988.
5   Sudjic, Deyan, "Return of the Master Builder", *The Sunday Times*, October 25, 1981.
6   Williams' first job was at the Victoria & Albert Museum, designing exhibitions under Roy Strong. For several years he was designing exhibition installations worldwide. The first commissions awarded to the practice were in this field, to which they made a significant contribution.
7   Stanton had been a key designer on the Pompidou Centre.
8   RIBA, June 21, 2006.
9   Amery, *Four London Architects.*
10 Holborn, Mark, *Issey Miyake*, Köln, Germany: Taschen, 1995.

COMPTON
VERNEY

Compton Verney is an eighteenth century Grade I listed mansion and estate in Warwickshire set within a Capability Brown landscape. Stanton Williams were commissioned to create an arts centre in, what had become by the late twentieth century, a near ruin. The exterior of the building was restored. Rooms within the mansion were refurbished where appropriate, and new 'rooms within rooms' were created where spaces were beyond repair. Display flexibility was maximised by building a new extension that, through its proportions and choice of materials, complements the existing mansion. The visitor experience and circulation were enhanced through careful planning of the flow of space between the three floors of galleries. Glass ramps, bridges and stairs were designed to link new and existing buildings and help capture the magical qualities of the natural light.

(Above) The new extension sits between the mansion and the cluster of outbuildings to the rear, including the Capability Brown Chapel.

(Opposite top) The west elevation of the new extension, with sculpture court, incorporates a remnant of the original out building's wall.

(Opposite bottom) Early design sketch for the east elevation of the new extension.

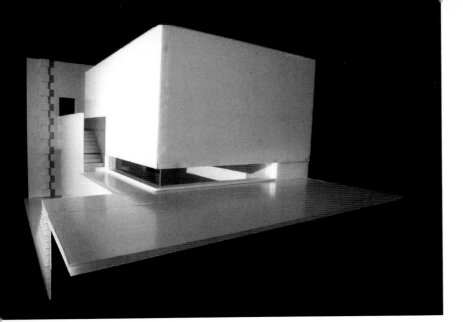

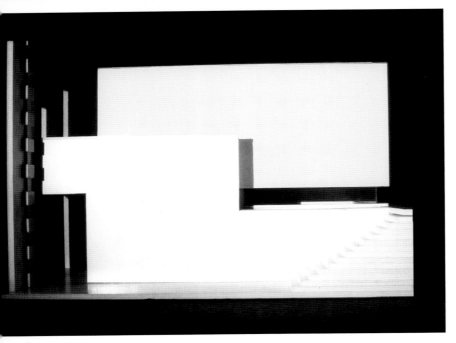

(Above) Study models of the
new extension set against the
north elevation of the mansion.

(Opposite) The limestone (Stoke
Ground) external walls of the
new extension echo the
appearance and texture of the
original house with contrasting
ashlar and tooled finishes.

(Overleaf) New extension, detail.

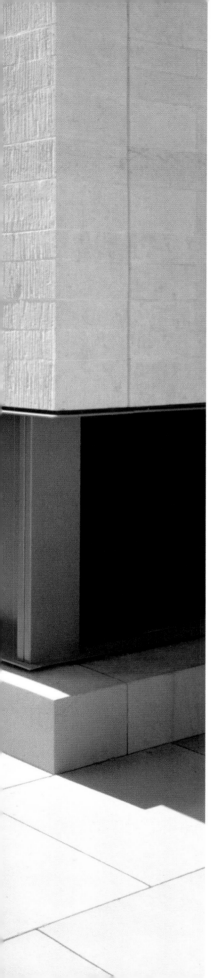

(Above) Glazed link separating new and old. Glass and steel ramp suspended between the tooled stonework of the mansion and the smooth fair-faced concrete of the new extension.

(Opposite) Detail of the etched glass ramp.

(Above) The new staircase faces a renovated dormer window of the mansion.

(Opposite) Located under a new roof light a staircase and lift were inserted into the mansion adjacent to the new gallery. Glass stair treads allow natural daylight to be drawn down into the building.

(Overleaf) Detail of the new doorway leading into the glazed link. The straight-grained European oak door and header are set within a powder-coated metal frame.

One of the mansion's principal
ground floor rooms before and
after restoration.

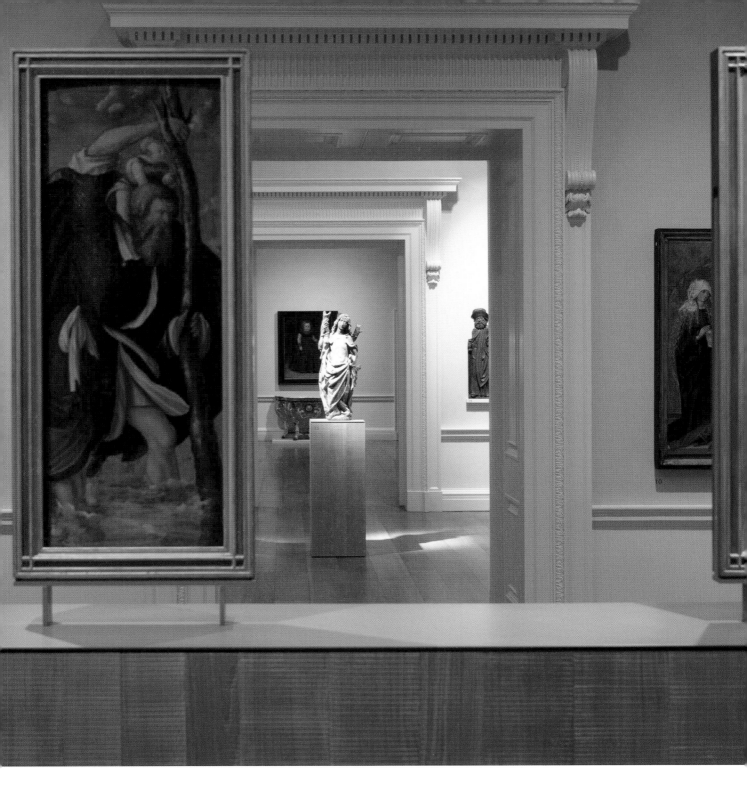

A typical first floor room. The requirement for environmental control necessitated a more radical intervention in all the rooms on the first floor of the mansion. A 'room within a room' strategy was adopted, with 'floating' moveable walls and ceilings concealing the control systems and ductwork. All visible existing doorways and walls retained their original features.

(Above) Photographs showing the design process that included card mock-ups of wall positions on site, and then developing the details by drawing over photographs.

(Above) Detail of limed oak display tables 'locked' into the floor plane.

(Opposite) The British National Folk Art Collection is displayed in the converted spaces at the top of the mansion.

(Opposite) The new
environmentally controlled
exhibition gallery on the first floor
of the new extension. This gallery
was created to provide a much
larger, flexible space for
temporary exhibitions.

(Overleaf) A timber-clad tunnel
connects the mansion and
extension to the new Education
Centre (built in the second phase
of the project).

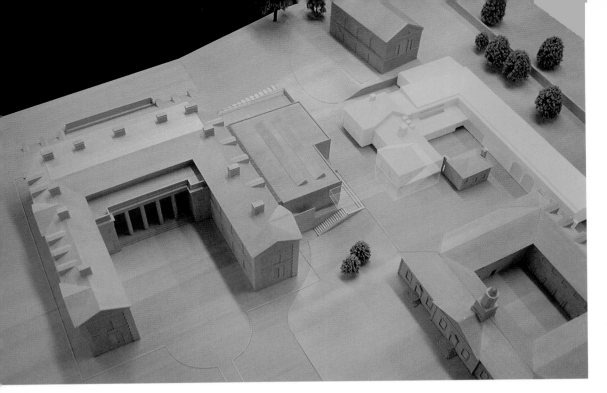

(Top) Model showing the extent of Phase II work—the creation of a new Education Centre set within an existing cluster of outbuildings.

(Bottom) Installation in the grounds of Compton Verney by artist Anya Gallaccio. Based on an original eighteenth century drawing by Robert Adam.

(Opposite) An open-tread staircase rises through the converted former Brew House (ground floor removed) connecting the new tunnel to the Education Centre on the upper level.

In Phase II, the new Education Centre and offices were created within a cluster of derelict outbuildings. The new building stitched together the outbuildings around a central courtyard.

(Top) View from the Education Centre building across a new brick-paved courtyard to the former Gun House and Coach House facade.

(Bottom) Children in the Education Centre.

(Opposite) The original Coach House arches are incorporated into the facade of the education centre building. A seminar room was created on the footprint of the old Coach House behind the arches.

(Above) New seminar space behind the existing Coach House arches. A north facing clerestory window maintains views of the orchards on the uppermost part of the sloping site.

(Opposite) Junction of the Education Centre and former Butler's Cottage.

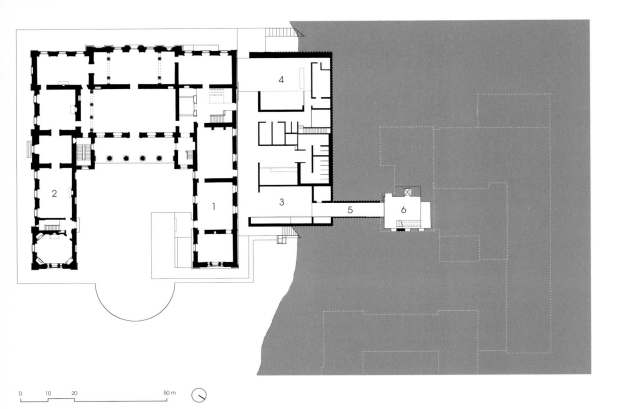

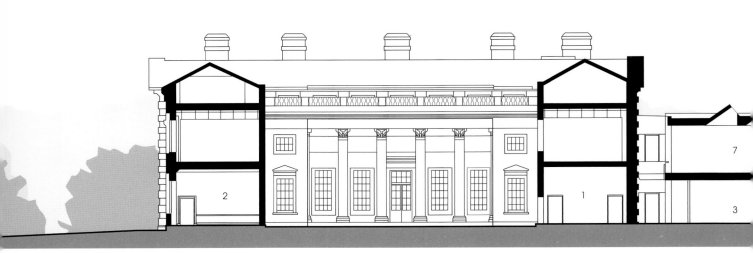

0 10 20   50 m

0   5   10   20 m

(Top) Ground floor plan.

(Opposite top) First floor plan.

(Bottom) Section.

1	Entrance		
2	Galleries	9	Butler's Cottage
3	Shop	10	Classrooms
4	Cafe	11	Seminar space
5	Tunnel	12	Artist in residence
6	Brew house and stair	13	Courtyard
7	New gallery space	14	Offices
8	Sculpture terrace	15	Orchard

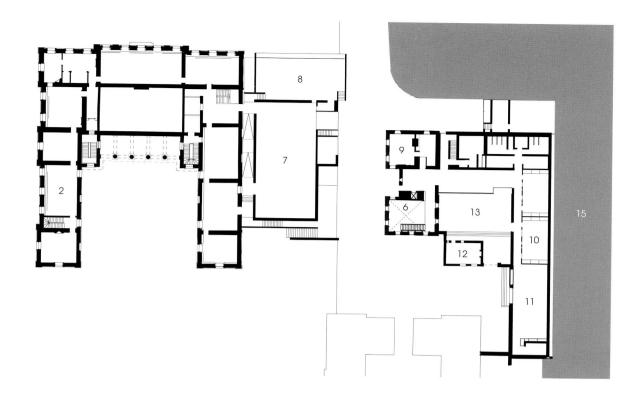

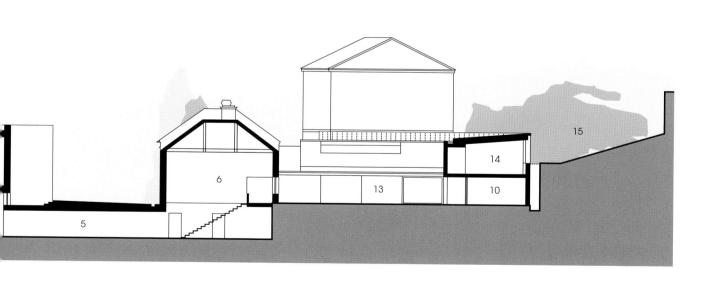

Compton Verney Art Gallery
Warwickshire, UK

Compton Verney is a Grade I listed country house, set within attractive countryside near Stratford-upon-Avon. Attributed to the co-designer of Blenheim Palace, John Vanbrugh, it was originally constructed in 1714. Robert Adam added new wings in 1760 and 1780, while the surrounding landscape was the work of the famed designer Lancelot "Capability" Brown. By the late twentieth century, however, the house had fallen into decay after decades of neglect and several changes in ownership. In 1993, Peter Moores acquired Compton Verney as a venue in which to showcase his extensive collection of art. After a design competition one year later, Stanton Williams was commissioned to develop design proposals. Completed in 2004, the result is an acclaimed public gallery, juxtaposing historic architecture with subtle layers of contemporary interventions and a sensitive approach to the landscape.

The brief was to transform Compton Verney from country ruin (included on English Heritage's register of Buildings at Risk) into art museum. Initial work analysed the history of the property, its strengths and weaknesses. In the resulting scheme, the character of the main house was maintained, its rooms becoming a series of galleries in which to display the permanent collections. A new building occupies the site of a long-disappeared service wing to the north, accommodating facilities that could not easily have been provided within the historic house without compromising its character, including a climate-controlled, flexible space for temporary exhibitions, as well as a shop, cafe, and toilets. The result is a sequence of spaces that offer an unfolding journey through post-Renaissance architectural history, from the High Baroque of the exterior to the contemporary expression of the new north wing.

Within the original house, the ground floor rooms were distinguished by their rich historic features, as befitted their original role as 'public' spaces for entertaining. These details were fastidiously repaired in collaboration with conservation architects Rodney Melville and Partners during the first phase of works, completed in 1998. The deep sash windows were retained, offering an ever-changing side light and views of the surrounding landscape. Floors were strengthened to take public gallery loadings, with the original boards being relaid above a sustainable heating system which draws warmth from the adjacent lake, while the existing doorways were carefully adapted to allow for the passage of large artworks. Almost all the galleries were painted off-white so as not to compete with the art displayed here, and to emphasise their airy proportions. The result is in many ways in the spirit of Adam's original scheme.

A different approach was taken within the first and second floor rooms, completed as part of a later phase of works in 2001–2004. The upper levels of the house lacked the architectural details of the ground floor, having originally been used as bedrooms and servants' quarters. In addition, a more interventionist approach to servicing was required. The idea emerged of these galleries as 'rooms within rooms', consolidating historic fabric where necessary but also positioning new panels in front of the original walls and ceilings to create additional display space. At skirting level and around openings, these panels step back to reveal the original walls, making clear their role as an inner skin within the permanent envelope of the original room.

The juxtaposition of old and new in the upper galleries offers a controlled transition between the historic house and the addition to the north. The result is a sense of abstraction, with the contemporary gradually taking precedence over the historic as visitors move from the ground floor rooms to the upper level to the extension. This relationship is made especially clear within a room on the north side of the house, where a new lift and stair have been inserted, offering full access to the whole building and reinstating a sense of order to the circulation which had been missing since the destruction in the late eighteenth century of the original principal stair.

Research revealed that there had originally been a service block to the north of the mansion, the disappearance of which had left an unsightly gap between it and the outbuildings beyond. By locating the new wing in this area, the first phase of the scheme reinstated the important relationship between the house and its setting, locking the building into the surrounding landscape. The bookshop, cloakroom, cafe and kitchens are located at ground floor level within the extension, with a flexible, environmentally-controlled gallery for temporary exhibitions above. Top-lit from the north, with slot glazing in its walls providing views of the gardens and the historic house, this gallery offers 225 square metres of space. It usefully complements those created within the original house in its flexibility, size, and in the degree of environmental control that it offers.

The desire to establish a creative dialogue between contemporary and historic architecture that shaped the approach to the interior of the original house also determined the treatment of the extension's exterior. The north wing, therefore, is highly contemporary in its cubic forms, making a distinct statement. At the same time, it is clearly subservient to the house in its position (set back from the corner pavilions) and its scale. The massing of the new wing closely responds to the adjacent elevation of the historic house, the vertical bands of which generate a rigorous order that controls the height of the extension and its various sub-elements including handrails and parapets. The use of stone echoes the appearance and textures of the original house, with contrasting smooth and tooled finishes catching the light in different ways.

The simultaneous connection and contrast between old and new is made especially clear in the inclusion within the new block of an earlier garden wall. Bookended and topped by new stonework, it reveals the two-storey glazed link which not only connects old and new but also serves to distinguish them. This link section itself is organised as a spacious promenade that functions as a spinal corridor at both levels, celebrating movement whilst offering a place for contemplation at the junction of old and new. A glass ramp and floor offer visual links between the different levels but also allow daylight to fall between new and old, emphasising their segregation. The contemporary expression of the 'new' side of this promenade contrasts visually with the rich textures of the north wall of the mansion on the other, scarred by weathering and the changes of centuries, but the two are linked in that each is controlled by rigorous geometries. In addition, the Baroque drama of the original house is reinterpreted in the glass floor of the upper level, which is cantilevered from the concrete of the new building, leaving a subtle gap adjacent to the wall of the mansion.

The second phase of works also included the addition of an education centre to Compton Verney within the derelict outbuildings located beyond the house. New blocks stitch these outbuildings together, creating a courtyard. A timber-clad tunnel leads to them from the main house and its extension, with the tunnel being connected to the courtyard above by means of a grand stair that rises dramatically through the full height of a former brewhouse. Within the education centre, external and interior space are linked by the use of brick for walls and floors, with large windows breaking down the distinction yet further.

In essence, Compton Verney is a story of relationships: between old and new; between the movement of people and the architectural frame that orders this movement; and between architecture and landscape.

CASA
FONTANA

Casa Fontana is primarily about space—a house that captures the almost infinite space of its setting—the lake, the city, the mountains. The villa is set on a southwest facing mountain slope, overlooking Lugano in the Swiss canton of Ticino.

(Above) Lugano and Monte San Salvatore from Aldesago.

(Overleaf) San Salvatore from the living room terrace.

(Left) The entrance, set between the house and the mountainside, leads to a double-height living room with stairs down to the dining room and lower terrace.

(Above) Double-height living room with fireplace and roof light above.

(Above and opposite) The dining room is separated from the kitchen area by a sliding white oak screen.

(Left) The lower stair in
travertino stone, is `carved'
into the hillside.

(Above) Beyond the lower stair,
light is drawn down through the
upper staircase void to illuminate
the guest bedroom corridor.

(Left) The upper (glass) stair is suspended above and disperses light down through the void.

(Above) Bathroom at the top of the house.

(Above) Pool with water cascade.

(Opposite) Dinning room terrace
and pool.

(Overleaf) The villa is conceived as
a sequence of interlocking forms
that sit against the slope of the site.

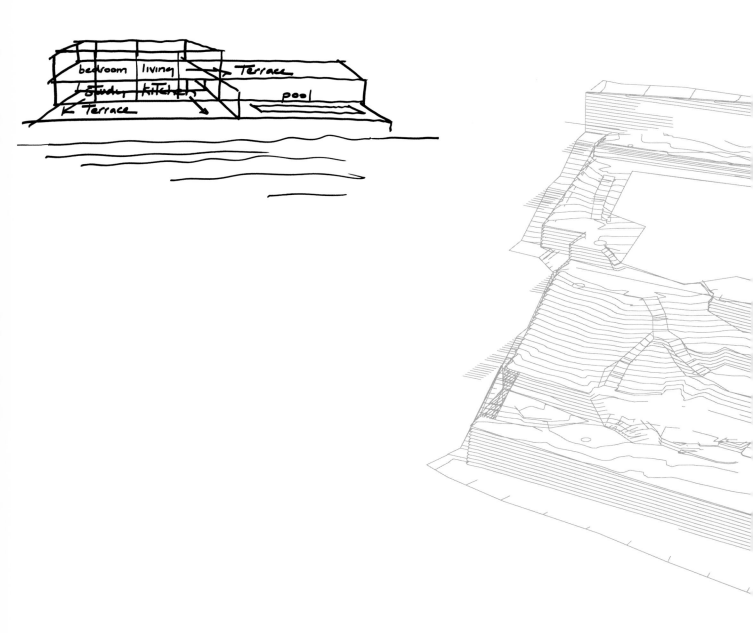

Walking the site for the first time with the client, he expressed his wishes in the form of a narrative: "I work in the cool of those shading pine trees there." "I make breakfast here looking this way." These vignettes were then strung together into a kind of 'living diagram' across the site.

(Above) The 'living diagram' drawn on the first site visit.

(Opposite) The three-dimensional survey drawing of the site shows the previous vineyard terraces. (Road access is at the bottom and the top of the site).

(Overleaf) Site plan and section through the garage/studio/pool.

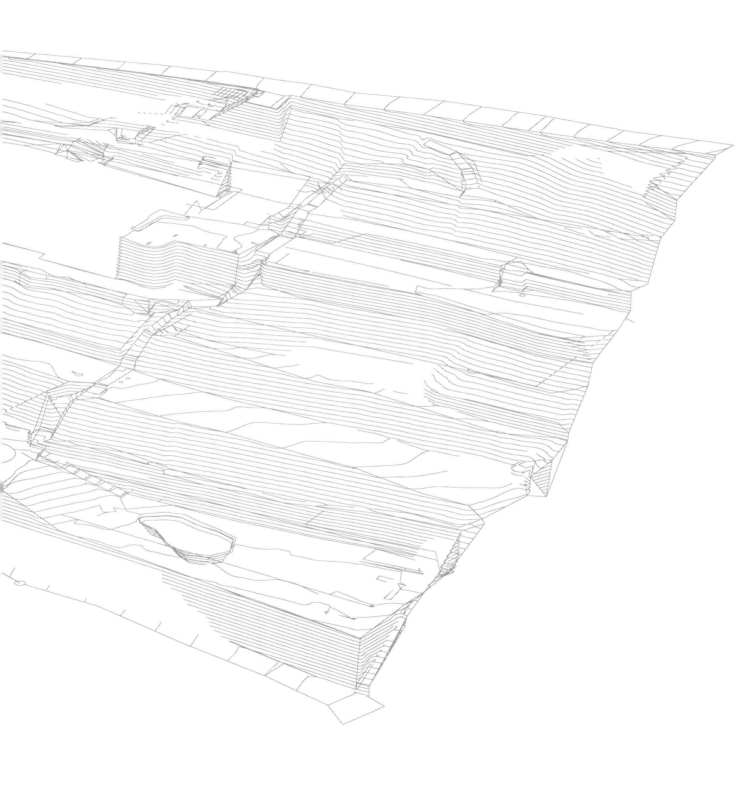

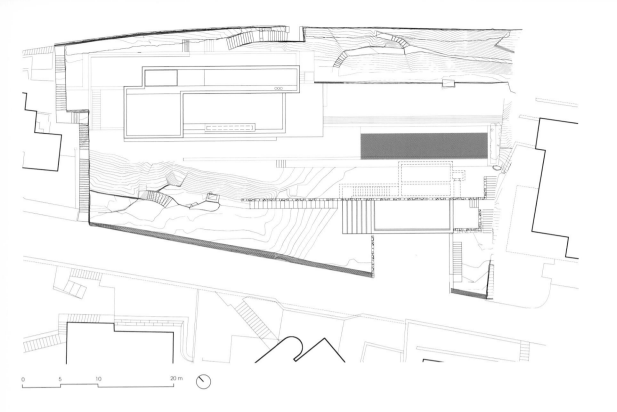

0   5   10   20 m

0   1   2   4 m

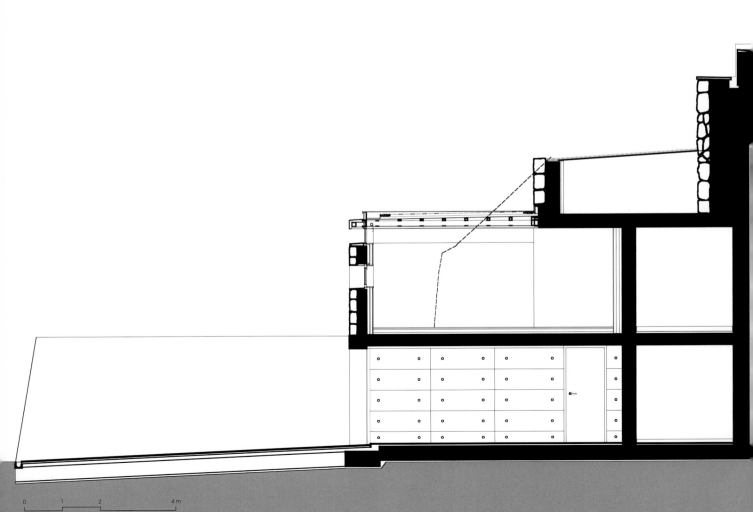

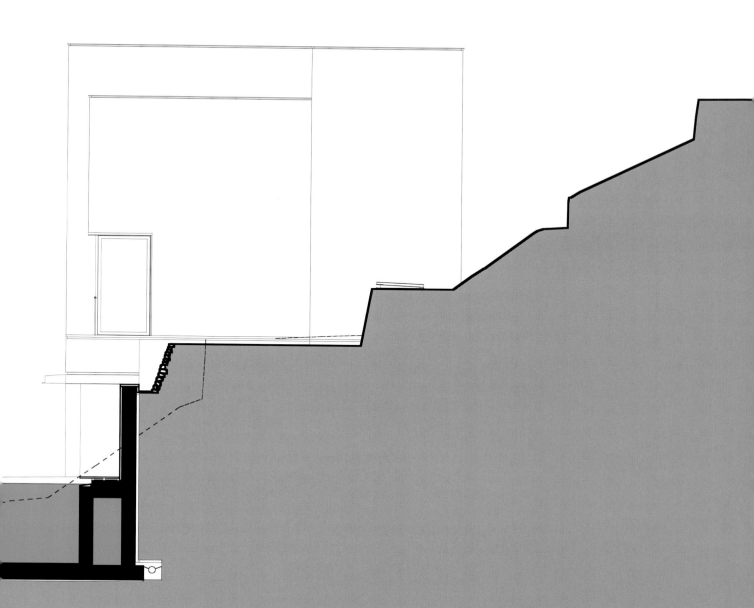

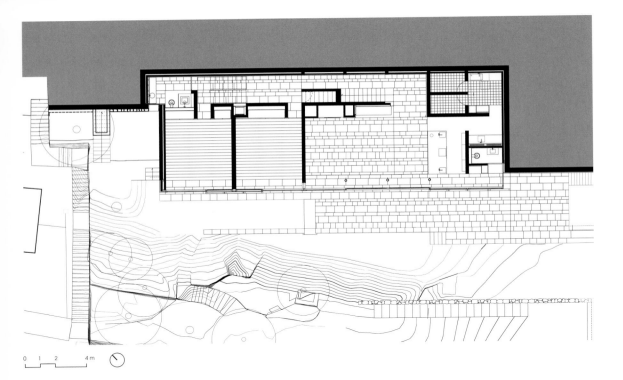

0   1   2   4 m

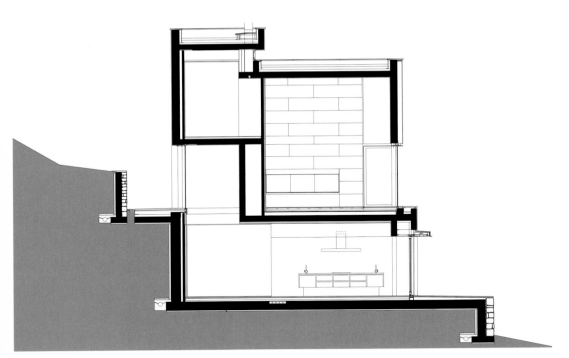

0   1   2   4 m

(Top) Dining room level plan.

(Bottom) Section through the
main house.

(Opposite top) Entrance/living
room level plan.

(Opposite Bottom) Upper
level plan.

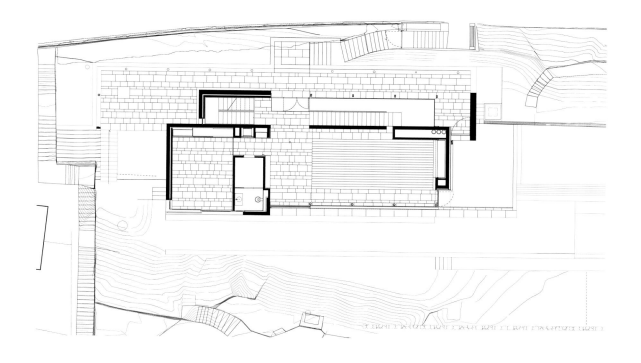

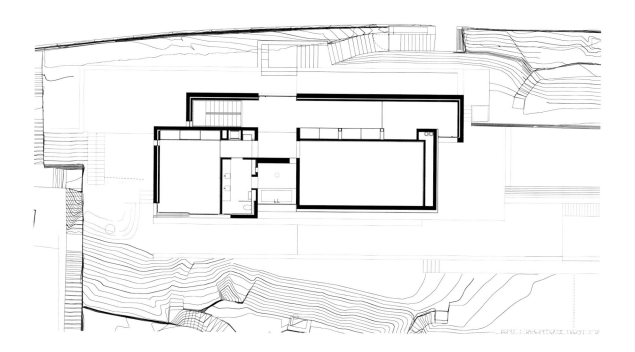

Casa Fontana
Lugano, Switzerland

Casa Fontana is primarily about space. The design sets out to capture its almost infinite Alpine setting, which is closely related to the landscape of the site and is then internalised within a sequence of domestic rooms.

The villa is conceived as a sequence of volumes that define its internal spaces, within which the human form is felt. Materials (stone, timber, metal) imbue the spaces with different qualities: warmth, coolness, activity, stillness. Details (shadow gaps and wall planes) offer definition and spatial linkages. Views are exposed, protected or framed, according to the function of the space from which they are seen, with closely framed openings for intimate rooms and generous panoramas for communal areas. The design takes account of the ever-changing light and weather conditions, and the need to provide warm or cool spaces.

Casa Fontana is located on a very steep terraced slope, in the village of Aldesago above the town of Lugano, and in the region of the lakes in the Swiss-Italian canton of Ticino. Orientated south west toward the lake, the villa has 180 degree panoramic views toward the Italian border of the Alps, Monte Rosa, Monte San Salvatore, Lugano and Melide. Ticino has a longstanding tradition of outstanding architecture and construction—from sixteenth century stone masons using their skills on famed Italian buildings, to a new generation of contemporary Swiss architects, via the work of the Baroque designer Borromini.

The landscape is distinctive. Located at the point where the Alps meet the Pô Valley, creating a cross between an Alpine and Mediterranean environment, the area is notably for the extreme variety of its plant species, from evergreens to palm trees. This luxuriant vegetation benefits from a microclimate of short cold winters and very hot summers, with an extended mild season.

The extraordinary nature of the site, a section of granite mountainside, challenged Stanton Williams to think about its topography and its geology. A road at its upper edge curves down past the site and then hairpin bends back along the bottom edge, suggesting a stepped promenade moving down through the site between the upper and lower road access points (like the fountain and water after which Casa Fontana is named). This promenade could then be expressed as a series of interconnecting layers, akin to strata carved into the rock.

Walking the site for the first time with the client, he expressed his wishes in the form of a narrative: "I work in the cool of those shading pine trees there", "I make breakfast here looking this way." These *vignettes* were then strung together into a 'living diagram' across the site.

Getting to grips with the problem of how to capture and relate the infinite spaces beyond the house necessitated a careful survey of viewing lines. Photographs and detailed measurements were used to establish angles and sequences across the site. The scale of the lake and the 80 kilometer view to the mountains could dominate any spaces that might be created and so the effort was to protect, frame, hold and even to obscure the views rather than to present conventional open panoramic vistas.

This sequence of manipulated views then suggested a series of locations, solids and open spaces relating to activities within the house—closely framed openings for intimate spaces, more generous apertures for communal areas. The entrance sequence expressed the contrast between open and closed at its most extreme. At the entrance door, accessed from a solid 'carved' space against the mountainside, views are withheld. On moving into the house, views are suddenly released, creating a sense of floating out over the lake and into the infinite space beyond.

Spaces are characterised by light and shade, and by temperature. The orientation of the site exposes the granite slope to the full effect of sunlight and heat during the afternoon. The 'compressed' space between the house and the rock is shaded during the day and cooled by the granite overnight. Light is drawn down through this space and scooped into the living areas. Coolness is brought to the open terraces with water. A cascade and pool are carved into the rock midway up the site, with the spatial quality reinforced by a lining of green granite. The pool's mirrored surface stretches out to the surface of Lake Lugano in the distance, reading as a single body of water.

The natural materials (travertino stone, white oak and granite) will weather gracefully and acquire a patina over time, allowing the house to blend with the landscape.

Commissioned by The Royal Botanic Gardens, Kew, for their estate at
Wakehurst Place in Sussex as one of the key millennium projects in the
United Kingdom, the Seedbank was designed to house a 'living library'
of over 300 million seeds. The building also contains laboratories, a visitor
centre and residential and academic facilities. Set within an Area of
Outstanding Natural Beauty (AONB), adjacent to a Site of Special Scientific
Interest (SSSI) on the Sussex High Weald, the building form and materials
were selected to minimise the building's impact on its surroundings.

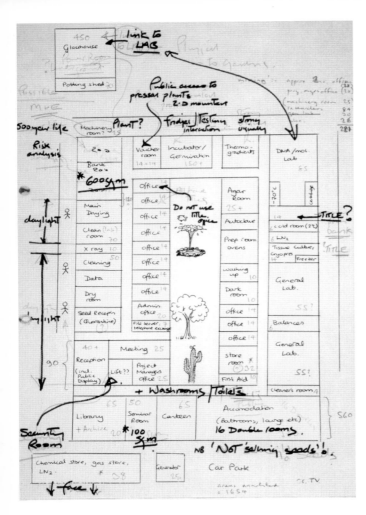

(Left) Initial sketch brief drawn by the scientists at Wakehurst Place, showing the laboratories and offices located around a private internal courtyard. Annotations in darker lines were made by Stanton Williams at the first client meeting.

(Opposite) The final design creates a more permeable layout, placing the laboratories around a central winter garden and creating space for a public exhibition. Yellow designates the public route and blue the seed route.

(Below) Taking advantage of the five metre fall in the natural contours of the site, the Seedbank itself is located underground, creating stable conditions and long-term security for its contents. Academic and residential facilities for visiting scientists are located around a sunken landscaped courtyard.

1 Winter garden
2 Laboratories
3 Seedbank
4 Seminar rooms
5 Bedrooms
6 Courtyard
7 Propagating glasshouse
8 Parterres

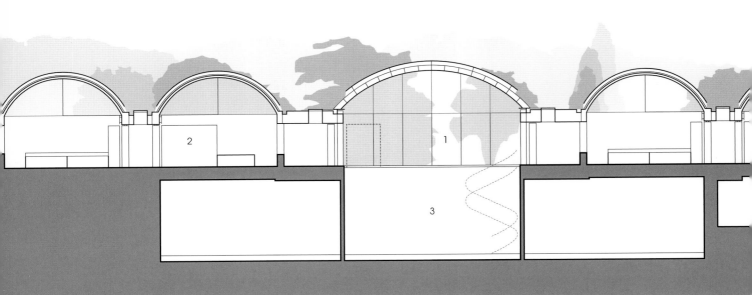

0 1 2   4m

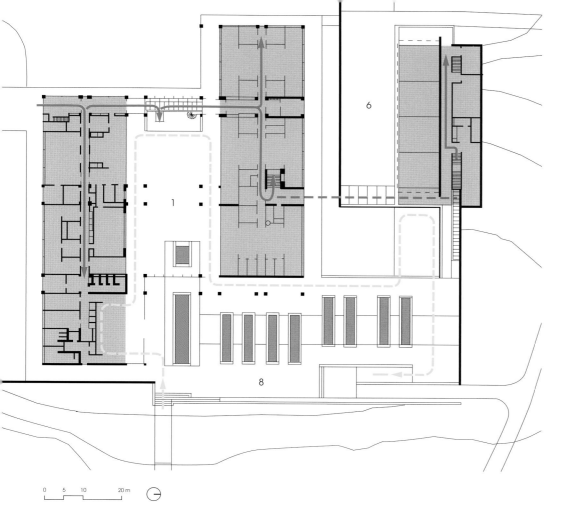

0 5 10   20 m

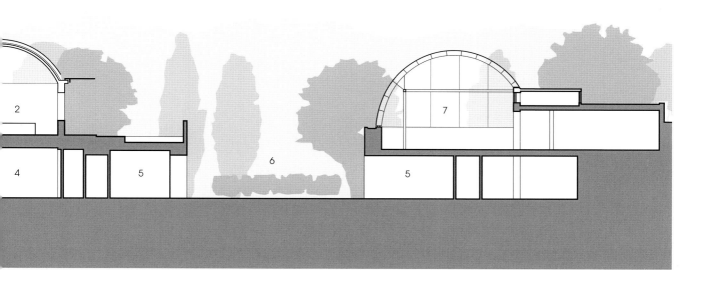

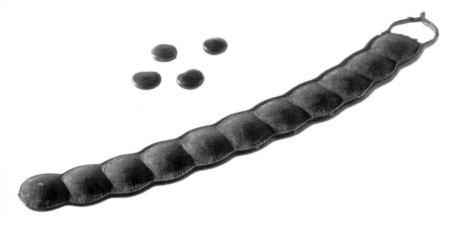

(Top) External views of the building set within the landscape.

The barrel-vaulted forms were designed to relate to the gentle curves of the landscape and local agricultural buildings.

(Bottom) The Seedbank's collection of over 300 million seeds vary in size from tiny grains to large seed pods, such as the Sea Bean (*Entada gigas*) some 100 cm long. The complex as a whole is, in its planning and form, somewhat akin to the seed pods of the Sea Bean in its undulating roof line and division. Its internal spaces are divided into a series of architectonic chambers.

(Right) The entrance courtyard with planted parterres leads through to the winter garden public area and connects to the landscape beyond.

(Overleaf) Winter garden exhibition space.

(Above) View of the exhibition space in the winter garden from the laboratories.

(Opposite) Fair-faced concrete ambulatory shading the scientific laboratories from direct sunlight.

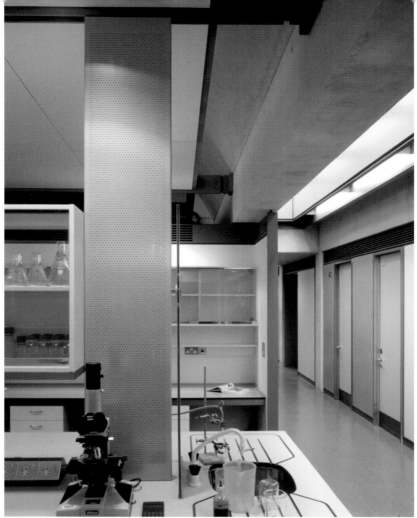

(Left) Glazed bridge at the western end of the winter garden links the laboratory buildings. A spiral stair and lift connect laboratories to the underground storage vault.

(Above) Laboratory interior and central corridor.

(Overleaf) Detail of the spiral stair.

(Above) The vaulted roofs overlook the parterres that display different UK ecospheres. A red brick wall, in the distance, redefines the boundary of the collection of buildings that make up Wakehurst Place. The textured 'split' sandstone coursing of the external walls reverts to a smooth ashlar finish as it engages with the sandstone paving.

(Opposite top) The propagating glasshouse.

(Opposite bottom) The academic wing with teaching and residential accommodation surrounding a lower private courtyard.

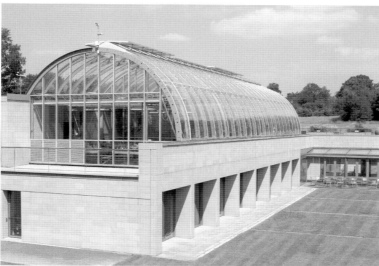

(Above) Full size card mock-up
being developed in the studio
showing the corner detail of the
concrete barrel vaults.

(Opposite) Section of the vaulted
roof. A zinc tern-coated stainless
steel layer sits above insulation
covering the vaulted concrete
shell. The dense, heavy concrete
of the barrel vaults are exposed
internally and act as a thermal
sink and moderate temperature
change.

Wellcome Trust Millennium Building
West Sussex, UK

One of the most ambitious international nature conservation projects ever undertaken, the Wellcome Trust Millennium Building (known informally as the "Millennium Seedbank") contains seeds representing nearly all the UK's flora. In total, there are some three million individual specimens. The Seedbank is rapidly developing its collections with the aim of holding ten per cent of the world's dry lands' flora by 2010. Completed in 2000, the complex sits in a beautiful landscape on the Sussex High Weald, its form and materials being intended to minimise the building's impact on its surroundings. The intention was to create an architecture which would express its functional purpose whilst simultaneously heightening the almost spiritual nature of the project, which, by gathering and storing seeds in the face of environmental change, has strong resonances of the Biblical Noah's Ark.

The Seedbank is located in the grounds of Wakehurst Place, a sixteenth century mansion. The estate is owned by the National Trust, but has since the 1960s been administered by the Royal Botanic Gardens, which takes advantage of the local microclimate and topography to grow plants which would not thrive at the main gardens in Kew. The brief set was for a building of 5,500 square metres to house the gardens' seed collections with space for research and conservation. It was to have its own identity as a significant research establishment whilst relating to the nearby existing service and residential buildings.

A schedule of accommodation prepared by the scientists at Wakehurst formed the basis of initial design development. This schedule proposed that laboratories and offices be located around an internal courtyard. The final design, however, represents a more permeable and flexible solution to the brief, placing the laboratories around a central winter garden and adding space for public exhibitions.

The design was developed with close reference to the site. Wakehurst's location within an Area of Outstanding Natural Beauty, adjacent to a Site of Special Scientific Interest, inevitably imposed a set of planning constraints, but the special nature of the site in any case suggested the need for a careful response. The Seedbank is 'grounded': it is a low-rise structure embedded quietly in the landscape and held by the line of the horizon. The design takes full advantage of the local topography. Not only is the site located on a spur ridge line that drops five metres from east to west, but the local sandstone layer is far below ground at this point, affording scope for a deep basement. Research, conservation and public areas are located above ground in a series of five parallel barrel-vaulted volumes, with the glazed public winter garden at the centre being flanked by laboratories. A similarly-vaulted greenhouse is set further to one side. To the north-west, taking advantage of the fall in the site, a sunken courtyard is ringed by academic facilities, including bedrooms for visiting scientists from overseas who come to the centre to learn about the seeds of their own country. The seed vault, meanwhile, is buried beneath.

The complex as a whole is, in its planning and form, somewhat akin to seedpods of the sea bean in its undulating roofline and the division of its internal spaces into a series of architectonic chambers (within which, laboratories may be easily 'plugged' and 'unplugged' as scientific method evolves). There are also resonances of local farm structures used to store the harvest, namely simple steel-framed sheds with corrugated metal vaulted roofs, while the post-and-beam structure recalls classical temple architecture, perhaps appropriately, given the spiritual qualities of the Seedbank project.

The sloping site brings visitors down to the main entrance. From the slope, there are views over the Seedbank's roof of the landscape beyond, and so a dramatic sense of arrival is complemented by an awareness of the building's setting. This relationship is developed yet further by the Seedbank's planning and materials. The building's main axis is set at right angles to the main house at Wakehurst Place, a relationship currently obscured by service blocks and trees but which could eventually be revealed in order to further lock the Seedbank into its setting. Throughout, the boundary between architecture and landscape is dissolved by means of glazed walls, views out, arcading, and abstract parterres. The effect is especially pronounced in the central winter garden, where glazing not only admits a constantly changing light but also gives a sense of the surrounding landscape entering the building and of the structure itself moving out into the landscape. In addition, similar forms permeate external and internal space. For example, the form of a raised granite pond at the entrance is reworked as a raised bed inside the winter garden, which, in stark contrast to the pond, contains plants from arid environments. Display cases take the theme further by again developing the form of the raised beds. Materials are carefully used. Thus the sandstone that has been used for the forecourt folds up into the elevations; the brick used for the parterres reflects the material of the perimeter walls.

The internal layout is shaped by the path that is followed by the seeds themselves, from initial processing to storage, research and germination. Glazing blurs the boundary between research areas and public space, allowing visitors to see scientists at work. Particularly dramatic in exposing the movement of seeds are views of the glass bridge which links the winter garden with the laboratories, and of the lift and spiral stair that connect the laboratories with the seed vault below.

Not only is the Seedbank itself intended to physically embody the idea of sustainability in storing seeds from the world's dry lands, where human existence is dependent on plants, but sustainable considerations significantly informed its design. Thermal mass, solar shading and natural ventilation are used wherever possible. The underground location of the seed store profits from the natural contours of the site in order to create stable conditions and long-term security for its contents. The dense heavy concrete of the barrel vaults above the laboratories acts as a thermal sink, removing the need for refrigerant cooling. Extracted heat from the cooling system used in the seed store is reclaimed for domestic hot water.

Jonathan Glancey, writing in *The Guardian*, described the Seedbank as "one of the very best of the millennium projects—architecturally, morally, intellectually, naturally". In its conception, the Seedbank reflects the underlying ambitions of the Millennium Commission to a significant degree through its aim to conserve the world's precious resources and advance scientific understanding of those resources. The building in which this activity takes place combines architecture and landscape, and, perhaps yet more significantly, offers in its balance of permanence and flexibility a sense of the natural world itself.

TOWER HILL

The project for Tower Hill, adjacent to the Tower of London (a World Heritage Site), won in an international competition in 1999, opens up the area to the west of the Tower as a new public square for London and the five million visitors each year who visit the site. The square provides new visitor facilities and links together the City, the River Thames and the historic Tower of London.

(Above) Aerial view of Tower Hill and the river from the south.

(Right) New Pavilions at the edge of the square form a colonnade and pedestrian promenade.

(Overleaf) View of the approach to the Square from the river jetty.

TOWER OF LONDON

↖ Tower Information
↖ Tower entrance
↑ Tower Pass Office
↑ Tickets

↑ Buses
← Taxi
↑ Trains

↑ All Hallows Church
↑ Telephone
↑ Toilets

(Above) The square from the western pavilion with Tower Bridge in the background.

(Right) The northern pavilion viewed from the moat-edge steps.

(Top) Granite bench with
integrated lighting.

(Bottom) Bench, detail.

(Opposite) Interpretation panels
at the edge of the square.

High quality paving and other materials add to the richness of the new square. The results are as much about 'place' as space, and the steps which link the promenade to the moat is an area that has successfully been used for theatre and other events, with the Tower itself as backdrop.

The clarity of the completed scheme belies the complexity of the project, which involved reconciling the rich archaeological and historic significance of the site with access legislation and the interests of the multiple groups involved.

(Left) Lighting benches at the edge of the square with the Thames in the background.

(Above) At night, the space is lit by bench lighting units and reflected light from the pavilion canopies.

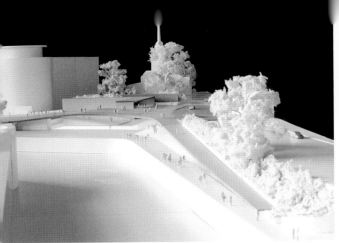

(Top left) The original competition-winning scheme opened up the public space of Tower Hill, and excavated beneath it to create a spacious curved volume for a visitor centre.

(Top right) When it was found unfeasible to carve into the hill (due to the later discovery of major underground service routes) a continuous pavilion was developed along the western edge of the new space. This was later vetoed by English Heritage.

(Bottom left) The final scheme with three pavilions visually linked by a colonnade.

(Opposite) site plan.

1 Tower of London
2 Moat
3 River Thames and jetty
4 Tower Place development
5 Moat ramp
6 Terrace steps
7 North pavilion
8 West pavilion
9 South pavilion

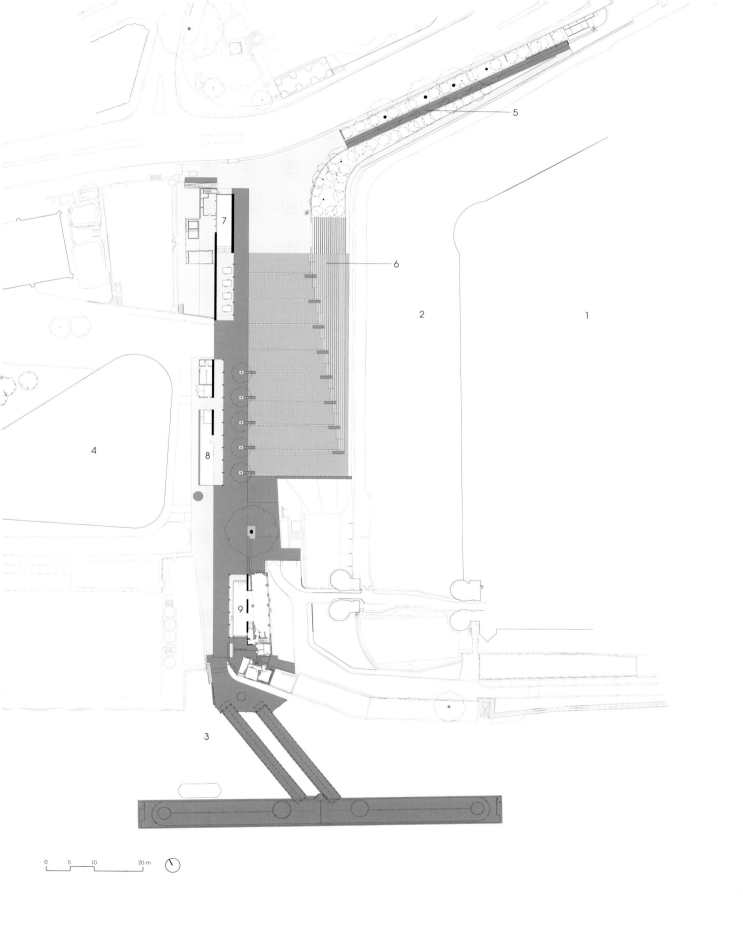

Tower Hill

London, UK

Historically, the Tower of London was surrounded by a large open area, free of buildings and planting. Known as "The Liberties", this empty space was intended to give those within a clear line of sight in case of attack. It also served to separate the Tower (whose later functions, similarly defensive, included prison and mint) from the city beyond. However, the need to cater for an increasing number of tourists from the mid-nineteenth century onwards and the removal of the Tower's traditionally introverted functions changed the nature of the site's relationship with its surroundings. The Liberties became a somewhat cluttered foreground, dominated by kiosks, bollards, mismatching paving, and facilities for taxis and coaches. Furthermore, much of the space to the west of the Tower was inaccessible, separated from its approaches by a substantial change in level and also divided by a road, while visitors arriving by Underground were sent to the riverside entrance via a narrow pavement and underpass, and then along the moat.

By the end of the 1990s, Historic Royal Palaces, the charitable body which manages the Tower, had resolved to take action. Permission was granted to close the road which ran through the area to the west of the Tower and a design competition was staged for new visitor facilities and a public square, directly accessible from the public approach route. Stanton Williams was selected from an international shortlist, and the new Tower Hill was opened by the Queen in July 2004.

The project vision revolved around clearing the area adjacent to the Tower and providing new locations for what was removed in a more coherent and consistent fashion than had previously been the case. At the same time, however, it presented the opportunity to create a significant new public space, roughly comparable in size with the central part of Trafalgar Square. Tower Hill is one of the few major public areas with direct riverfront access in the City of London. Sensitive handling was thus necessary if the result was to convey a sense of 'place' as well as 'space'.

With the accretions removed, the open space to the west of the Tower was reworked as a promenade, falling gently and without interruption from the main road and Underground station at the northern end of the site to the river and Tower entrance at the south. As visitors arrive, they are treated to a spectacular view of the Tower before they descend the slope to reach its entrance. Carefully negotiating the rich archaeological significance of this area, the slope's unbroken nature results in an organic sense of 'place' rather than created 'route', as would have been the case had there been the intermediate landings and railings that a steeper slope would have necessitated.

Necessary facilities for visitors are provided along the western edge of the promenade. Two new pavilions define the boundary along its upper reaches and house the Welcome Centre and Ticket Office. The Ticket Office is connected to the stump of a warehouse, destroyed in the Blitz apart from its multiple basements and a solitary above-ground storey. The line of the two pavilions is continued at the lower end of the promenade by an extension to 'Salvin's Pumphouse', a characterful Victorian Gothic survivor which now houses the Shop. The architectural language of the pavilions and the Pumphouse extension is consistent, using steel, glass, granite and a rectilinear geometry to create a permeable transparency which contrasts with the introverted solidity of the Tower itself. Each offers a colonnade towards the promenade, recalling such historic examples of public squares edged by covered ways as the Greek agora. The colonnades' role here is especially important: on busy summer days, visitors can spill out into the square; on wet winter days when numbers are lower, they offer an appropriate shelter.

The difference in levels between the ever-rising promenade and the consistent height of the adjacent moat-side walk is mediated by a flight of steps, parallel with the moat. As the steps turn at right angles onto the surface of the promenade, they become granite benches. Both the benches and the steps form a popular and informal sitting area. They have been used on occasion as a venue for theatrical performances, with the moat and Tower functioning as an impressive backdrop.

Particular attention was paid to the quality of materials and finishes deployed: it was imperative that the paving, for example, did not crack under the weight of the occasional delivery lorry or refuse truck. Ensuring a clutter-free environment was also an important concern. There is minimal street furniture: no bins, signs, or lamp posts. Lights are set within the paving or the benches which seemingly grow out of the steps, and there is virtually no planting within the square itself, unusually for post-Victorian public space. In this respect, Tower Hill recalls earlier notions of urbanity, as well as the emptiness of the original Liberties, and forms an appropriate setting for the Tower, complementing rather than competing with it.

Achieving this result involved lengthy negotiations with four funders, two local authorities, and a vast spectrum of amenity and interest groups. The project had to respect and respond to the constraints imposed by the historic buildings on the site, as well as the below-ground limitations resulting from the site's wealth of archaeological remains. The massive optical fibre cables which connect London's financial centre with the world pass below the promenade, adding another constraint which limited the extent of subterranean excavation. The apparent simplicity of the executed solution, as a place, and in the scale and detail of the buildings, belies the effort and attention given to the project.

BELGRADE THEATRE

As spectators gather, they surround the performer in a semi-circle, then a full circle. Children will crawl through and sit in front. As the crowd grows denser, those at the perimeter might climb into a tree or onto a balcony.

The project for the Belgrade Theatre, Coventry provides the Theatre with a second auditorium, expanded foyers and extensive backstage facilities. The volume for the new theatre space was developed from a study of the scale and proportions needed to achieve an 'intimate' relationship between stage and audience.

(Above left) Crowds naturally form spaces around the performers on the piazza at the Centre Pompidou, Paris.

(Above right) Trees are appropriated by spectators.

(Right) The architecture exists to support the spectacle. Sketch for the (later superceded) timber horseshoe auditorium for the Belgrade.

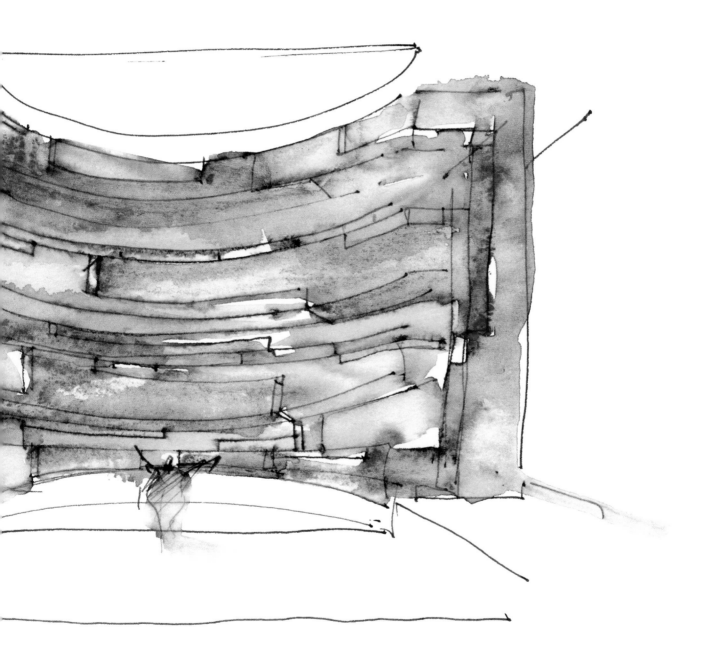

(Above) The Belgrade (B2)
auditorium. A flexible 'kit of parts'
that sits within the concrete 'cube'
volume of the new building.

(Right) The new entrance foyer
and cantilevered balcony.

The ramped entrance space, a
'fissure' created by drawing apart
the two major volumes of the new
building, draws light and people
through it on three levels.

(Opposite) The building viewed
from the entrance courtyard.

(Overleaf) The facades are
expressed with render finishes
of different colours and textures.
Above a back-lit translucent
screen articulates the plant
room as a volume.

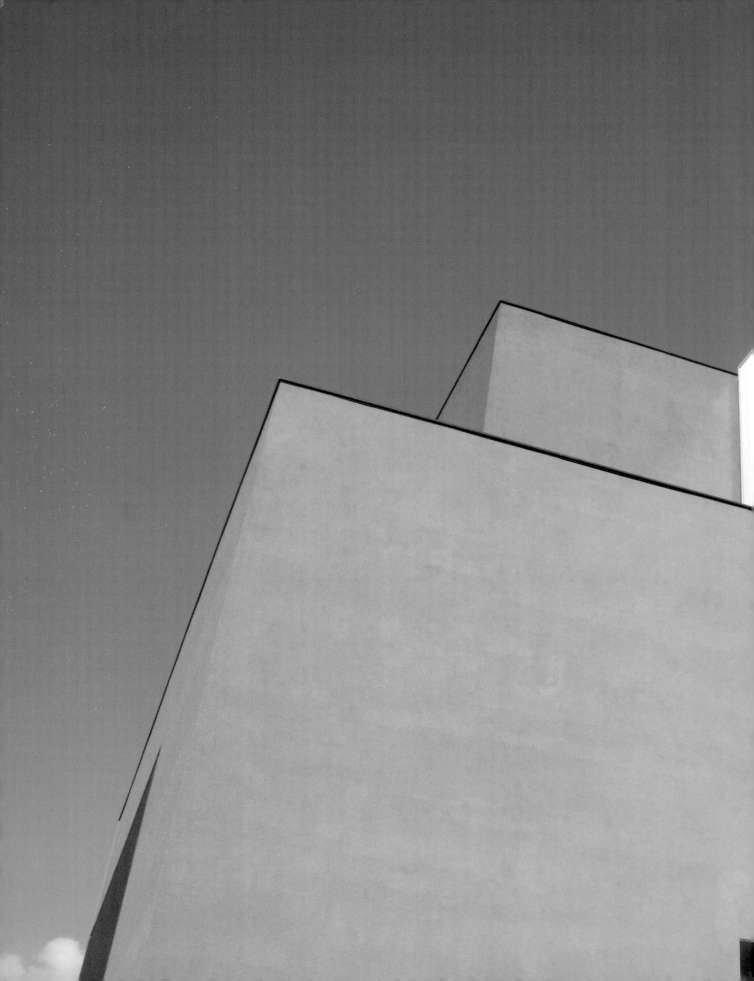

The new building is strongly vertical, contrasting with the lower-slung horizontals of the original theatre. Through the combination of differently-sized volumes plus the contrasting use of coloured renders and translucent panels, it functions as a beacon that signals the Theatre's presence within an evolving cityscape and responds to the scale of an adjacent new mixed-use development. Inside, the new foyers connect with the 1958 public spaces, which have been stripped back to their original appearance. The (B2) second auditorium is a flexible space which can be used in various configurations. Wrapped around it are new dressing rooms and technical spaces, whilst above is the theatre's first purpose-built rehearsal room.

(Opposite top) The new building against the backdrop of Coventry's city centre.

(Opposite middle) Early sketch of the building as viewed from Coventry's Ring Road.

(Opposite bottom) Development sketch of the building.

(Above) View of the entrance courtyard, B2 theatre volume and rehearsal room/plant volume.

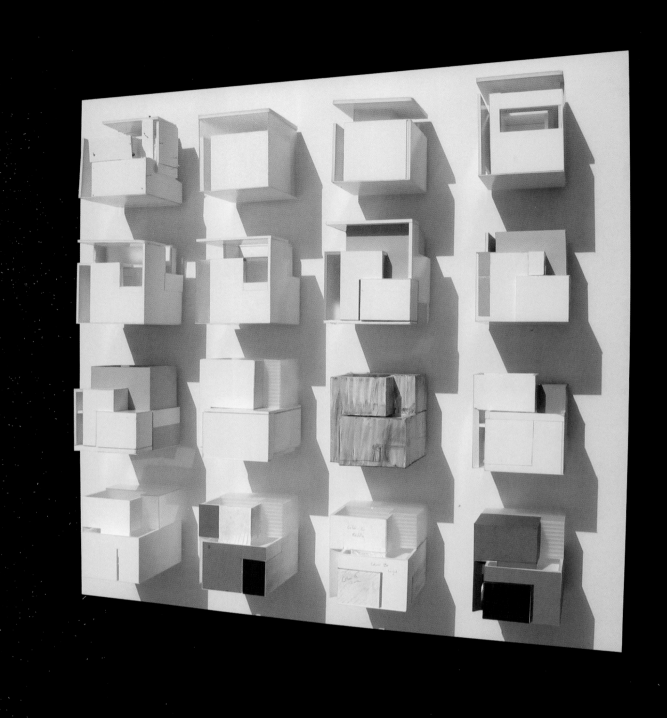

(Above) A sequence of sketch
models shows the design
development of the building's
form and spaces.

(Opposite) Final sketch model.

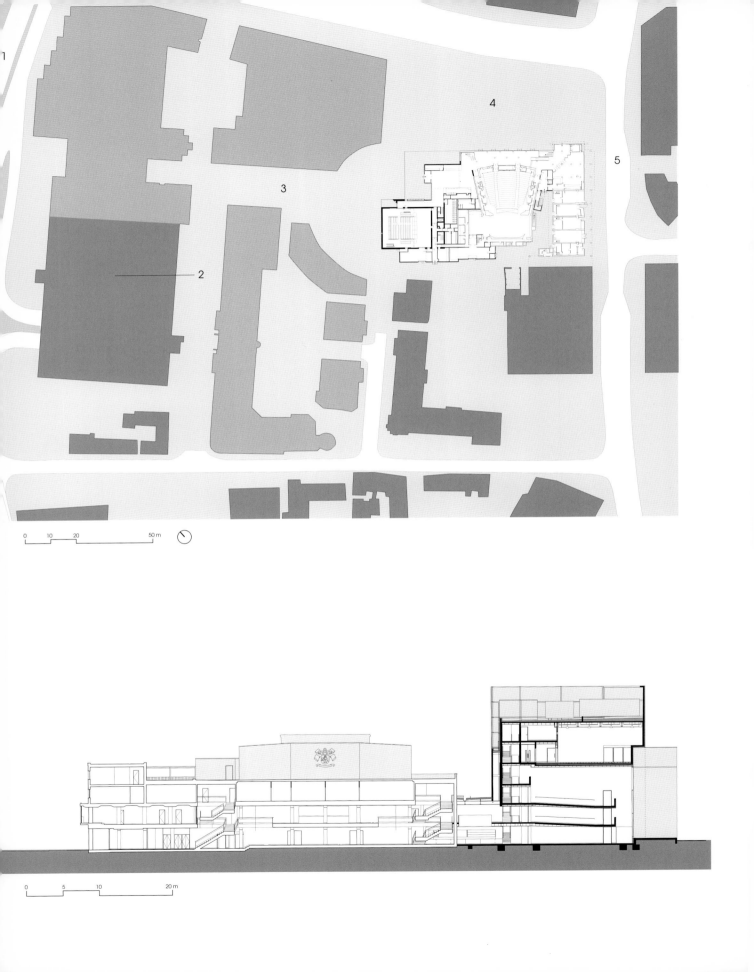

1

3

2

4

5

0 10 20   50 m

0 5 10   20 m

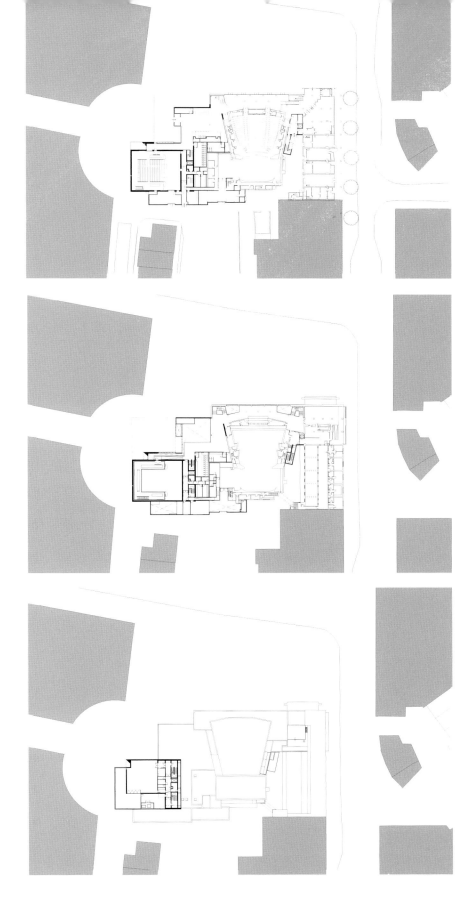

(Opposite top) Site plan.

1   Ring road
2   Car park
3   New Belgrade Plaza
    development
4   Belgrade Square
5   Corporation Street (city centre)

(Opposite bottom) Section through
the new and existing building.

(Right) Ground floor plan/First
floor plan/Third floor plan.

Belgrade Theatre
Coventry, UK

When it opened in 1958, Coventry's Belgrade Theatre was the first all-new professional theatre to be built in Britain for 20 years, and the country's first purpose-built civic theatre. The building represented a new age, that of the subsidised, democratic theatre, while the artistic programme won acclaim for its willingness to tackle subjects not hitherto much seen on British stages. By the turn of the twenty-first century, however, the Theatre's facilities were proving inadequate. Stanton Williams was commissioned in 2002 to provide the Belgrade with a second auditorium, expanded foyers, and improved backstage facilities. The results complement the restored Grade II-listed modernism of the original whilst at the same time giving Coventry a bold contemporary landmark.

A second auditorium had long been the goal of the Theatre's management, who sought a flexible space in which they could stage small-scale productions unsuited to the size or format of the original 850 seat, proscenium arch auditorium. A foundation stone had, in fact, been laid in the 1960s by Sir Laurence Olivier, but it was only at the beginning of the twenty-first century that the Belgrade was able to raise the necessary funding to begin work. The Theatre was also keen to improve its backstage accommodation, which had never been truly adequate: dressing rooms and technical areas were cramped, plus there was no purpose-built rehearsal room. And while the Belgrade's public foyers had been among the most spacious ever seen in Britain when they opened in 1958, they had become somewhat tired in appearance, with their crisp 'Festival of Britain' modernism having been obscured by layers of unsympathetic accretions. Interventions were also necessary to address the requirements of Health and Safety legislation, as well as accessibility guidance.

The Theatre extension forms a bridge between the original building and a mixed-use development to its west. With seven storeys, it is strongly vertical in emphasis, contrasting with the lower-slung horizontals of the original building. The design comprises interlocking cubic volumes of black and grey render, red panels, glass, and translucent plastic. The coloured renders and the use of window 'slots' break up what would otherwise be the large, unrelieved surfaces necessitated by the auditorium within.

The relationship between the Theatre and its surroundings is critical to the conception of the scheme. The Theatre's original main entrance faces a small public square at the junction of Corporation Street and Upper Well Street, but in recent years most patrons had arrived by car, using the rear doors in order to enter the building from a nearby multi-storey car park. The extension occupies this area, with a new glazed elevation offering a more inviting and spacious entrance than the gloomy vestibule of the previous rear door. When the adjacent development is completed, this elevation will form one side of a new semi-circular public space.

Patrons entering by means of the new entrance arrive in a double-height galleried space which houses the box office and bar, and gives direct access to the new auditorium. It connects seamlessly with the 1958 foyers, which have been stripped back and sympathetically restored. The external colour palette of grey, black and red is used throughout the foyers. In this respect, not only are interior and exterior connected, but so too are new and historic architecture. Attention was given to achieving an appropriately 'theatrical' atmosphere in such elements as the glossy red finishes applied to the bar, or the staircase lighting, which creates dramatic pools of illumination.

The galleried arrangement of the space adds to this atmosphere in emphasising the drama of the gathering audience by means of views between the different levels. The result is a significantly larger and more inviting place in which to gather, not only at performance times but also whenever the building is open during the day.

The new second auditorium is a flexible space which can be used in various configurations: end stage, in-the-round, or courtyard theatre. It was originally conceived as a 'piece of furniture' within a fixed 'room', recalling the construction of such Renaissance theatres as the Teatro Farnese at Parma, where a tiered wooden seating structure sits within a larger volume. This idea was set aside during the design process in response to the emerging wish of the Theatre's newly-appointed director for a more adaptable auditorium. However, the result still recalls the original concept to some extent: the auditorium and stage structure are inserted within the concrete envelope of the surrounding building. With galleried seating around its edges, removable stalls at the lowest level, and movable gantries flying above the space, the result is an adaptable framework for performance. Wrapped around it are new dressing rooms and technical areas, including the Belgrade's first purpose-built rehearsal room.

Just as the construction of the Belgrade Theatre in the 1950s was intended to make a statement about the place of the arts in post-war Britain, so too was this project conceived as a statement of the Belgrade's renewed confidence, as well as that of Coventry's as a whole. Soaring above the original building, the extension functions as a clear signpost of the Theatre's presence within an evolving cityscape, and of its ambitions for the future.

DEPARTMENT STORE

Completed in September 2008, the department store for House of Fraser in Bristol anchors the new Cabot Circus shopping centre. It offers a contextual response to the city with a careful use of organic, tactile materials. The treatment of glass and bronze—traditional department store materials—was developed in close collaboration with artist Susanna Heron. The result is a fusion of architecture and art whose contextual basis seeks to be both contemporary and timeless.

(Above) Cast bronze panels with a milled and 'molten' cast surface, are juxtaposed with smooth copper cassettes which, like the bronze, will acquire a deep patina over time.

(Opposite) Roach Bed Portland stone with a fossil rich surface, seen through a sand-blasted and acid etched art glass panel.

The building comprises massive cubic volumes at its upper levels, juxtaposed and cantilevered out above a single-storey plinth. Their dynamic sculptural form recalls shifting tectonic blocks, an impression reinforced by the fossil-rich Roach bed Portland stone with which they are predominantly clad. Large windows and narrow vertical glazed 'faults' punctuate the stonework, adding to the sense of movement and allowing views out. Those at the corners appear not as lightweight openings, but rather as solid, reflective blocks by day and beacons of light at night, signalling the store's presence at the gateway to the city.

(Opposite and above)
Views of the building from Bond Street.

The west elevation of the building.

Views into and out of Cabot Circus
shopping centre.

(Above) The department store
seen from the shopping centre.

(Opposite) The internal atrium
and escalators.

The second floor restaurant
looking out through the
etched art glass window.

(Above) The first example
of the bronze panels laid out
in the workshop.

(Opposite) Drawings for the
etched glass panels in Susanna
Heron's studio.

(Top) Early models exploring
the potential of the cantilevered
volumes at the upper levels,
recalling the imagery of shifting
tectonic blocks.

(Bottom) Watercolour images
expressing the building as an
animated sequence of
unfolding abstract elevations.

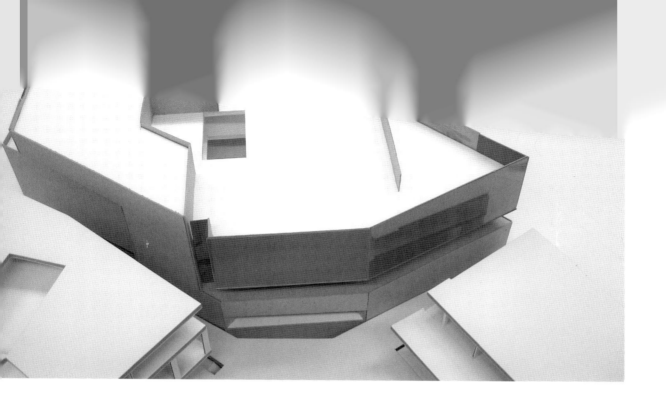

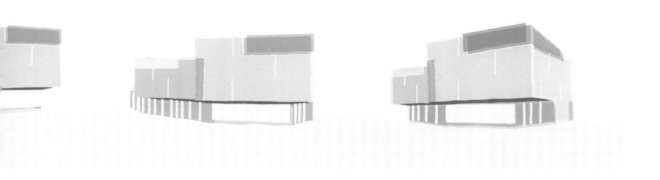

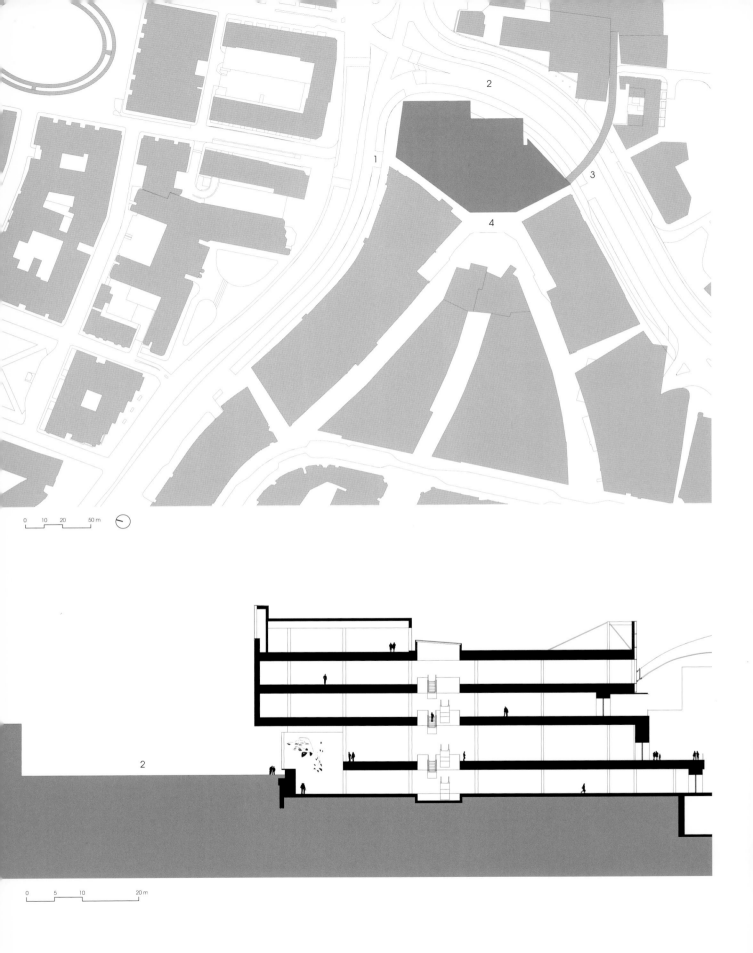

0 10 20   50 m

1

2

3

4

2

0 5 10   20 m

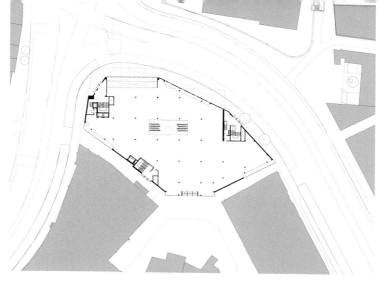

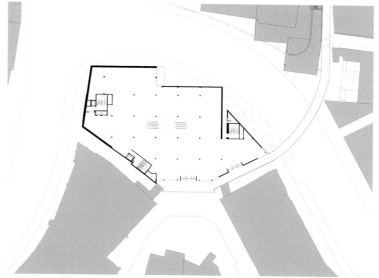

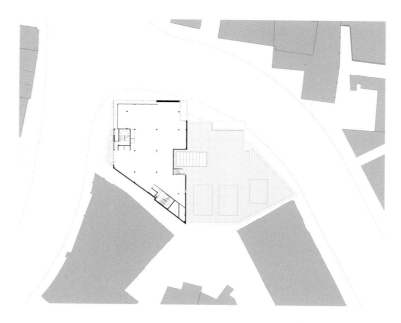

(Opposite top) Site location plan.

1 Newfoundland Street
2 Bond Street
3 Bridge link to car park
4 Shopping centre

(Opposite bottom) Section.

(Right) Ground floor/First
floor/Third floor plan.

Department Store
Bristol, UK

Completed in September 2008, House of Fraser in Bristol anchors the new Cabot Circus development, a shopping area which is intended to breathe fresh life into a hitherto run-down part of the city centre. The design was conceived as a dramatic landmark, visible for some distance and not only anchoring Cabot Circus but also marking the entrance to the city centre. At the same time, the building is intended to create interest at the scale of the passing pedestrian or motorist by virtue of its sculptural form and the tactile nature of its surfaces, developed in collaboration with the artist Susanna Heron. It challenges the banality of much retail architecture and the current preference for iconic 'black-box' stores, unrelated to their surroundings and perhaps transient in their fashion. Instead, the design seeks to connect with the urban landscape of Bristol, whilst also reinterpreting the traditional nineteenth century department store by means of its materials and detailing.

Cabot Circus extends and draws together the three parallel streets of the 1950s Broadmead shopping area as a series of new semi-covered spaces onto which face buildings by various architects. At the focal point where the three converging arcades meet, the masterplan envisaged an 'anchor' store, for which Stanton Williams was appointed. Rather than viewing the elevation which faces into the shopping area as the principal facade, and the rest, facing the surrounding streets, as the rear, the design treats the entire envelope as a principal elevation. Its appearance is intended to enliven the locality and to fulfil the brief that this building would signal arrival in the city.

The northern and eastern boundaries of the site are formed by the curving line of Bond Street, with a busy junction at the north-eastern corner. Rather than present a continuous facade literally emulating the street line, at pavement level the building instead comprises a series of short, straight sections (drawn as chords across the curve). This jagged edge provides pedestrians and motorists with views which shift and alter depending on the angle of approach whilst also creating interest by revealing the streetscape in unfolding stages. The upper storeys consist of massive cubic volumes, arranged independently of the pavement-level plinth and, in fact, dramatically overhanging it at points. Their dynamic, sculptural form recalls shifting tectonic blocks sliding past each other, thrust out of the ground. This geological allusion is reinforced by the strata-like 'gap' between the lower and upper parts of the elevation and by the treatment of the facades themselves.

Above plinth level, the elevations are largely clad in stone-faced precast concrete panels, arranged in portrait format. The largest is nearly two by ten metres in size. The geological theme suggested by the building's massing is developed in the use of Roach Bed Portland stone as the principal facing material. Hard and durable, Roach is noteworthy for its high fossil content: where the shells within the stone have long since decomposed, there are now holes—negatives, or moulds, in effect—which imbue it with a lively, textured appearance. At the main corner of the building, smoother Whitbed stone is used, contrasting with the Roach in the way that it is caught by the light and in its appearance when wet. The impression is akin to a textured garment worn smooth at a certain point by frequent contact.

The stone volumes are broken up at intervals by 'faults', namely slots that are either glazed or artificially lit and which create the impression of further movement. At the corners of the volumes, large glass panels are deployed flush with the stonework. They appear not as simple lightweight openings, but rather as solid, reflective blocks by day and beacons of light at night. This is especially true of the translucent section that is located at the highest corner and which is visible for some distance. The panels' contrast with the surrounding stonework further accentuates the sense of tectonic plates sliding across each other. More tangibly, they allow views from the building by day and views in at night, orientating shoppers and avoiding the dislocation of the typical black-box, while the vast double-height display window at the Bond Street junction is critical in giving the building an active frontage at plinth level.

The organic, tactile theme introduced by the Roach Bed stone is continued in the palette of materials used elsewhere on the building. The plinth level features panels of bronze, weighing up to 160 kilograms. These panels were deliberately cast to produce a rich texture with as much variation and relief as possible—each one is unique. The effect could be conceived in terms of molten metal, perhaps forced out of the earth by tectonic shifts; the result, like the Roach, is a surface which catches the light in varied ways and which people want to touch—another kind of active frontage. The panels are juxtaposed with smooth copper cassettes, which, like the bronze, will acquire a deep patina over time.

The treatment of the bronze panels was developed by the artist Susanna Heron. She sought to develop the ideas of negative relief and life suggested by the fossil-rich stonework, and so 27 panels are partly milled smooth according to her instructions. The sinuous edge of the junction between the smooth milled surface and the untreated textured areas again recalls the idea of molten metal. In places, the cast surface is dropped below the level of the milling, creating a negative texture akin to the fossilised stone. Heron was also involved in the treatment of the largest glazed section in the upper volume, a vast surface six metres tall by 14 wide that is uninterrupted by internal floors. Each of its panes was individually sand-blasted and acid etched by hand to a unique organic pattern of her design. The technique, which had never before been used on this scale in the UK, creates an incredible dappled effect. By day, natural light shining through this glazing casts shadows and forms internally; by night, the window projects patterns onto the surrounding external walls. As with the bronze panels, this window represents a very real, natural collaboration between artist and architect which elaborates and extends the guiding themes of the design. It is not the application of art to an already completed architectural vision.

In some ways, the attention given to materials and detailing in this project has been conceived as being akin to a bespoke *couture* garment. But the combination of natural stone, glass, bronze and public art also allows the building to be understood as the contemporary reinterpretation of the grand department stores of the late nineteenth century. In this way, in the building's organic response to its setting, and in its interaction with its users, the design aims to be at once contemporary and timeless.

SPACES
FOR ART

In 1706 Queen Anne gave to the Abbey the
baroque marble altarpiece made for her father's
Roman Catholic chapel in Whitehall Palace.
It was a work of exceptional quality, designed
by Sir Christopher Wren and adorned with
sculptures by Arnold Quellin and Grinling
Gibbons. The two angels exhibited here flanked
a symbol of the Holy Name at the top of the
structure. Although different in style from the
Gothic monuments around the apse, the scale
of the altarpiece and its fine materials made it
a worthy focus at the heart of the Abbey. It was
discarded at the Coronation of George IV. Some
pieces, including the angels, went to Burnham-
on-Sea in Somerset, where they formed part of
a reredos until the late 19th century.

(Pages 220–222)
Bridget Riley,
Tate Britain, 2002.

(Pages 223–225)
Yves Klein,
Hayward Gallery, 1994.

Triforium Gallery,
Winchester Cathedral, 1992.

(Opposite)
Design Museum Galleries,
detail, 1989.

(Overleaf)
Spectacular Bodies,
Hayward Gallery, 1999.

Ancient Art of Mexico,
Hayward Gallery, 1992.

**Seduced: Art and Sex
from Antiquity to Now**,
Barbican Gallery, 2007.

(Above and opposite)
Gerhard Richter Portraits,
National Portrait Gallery, 2009.

(Overleaf)
**Leonardo da Vinci: Experience,
Experiment and Design**,
V&A Museum, 2006.

Making Things
Building

Leonardo performed many roles and undertook many tasks for his court patrons. He performed many of his duties with enthusiasm. However, they took him away from the making of paintings and sculpture, upon which he pinned most of his hopes for fame.

Architecture was the most prestigious of these activities. He developed an innovatory vision of architecture as a way of shaping space. He depicted buildings as sculpted forms and as solid sections. He designed canals and basins as settings for buildings.

Each part of a Leonardo building obeys the rules of proportion. He investigated the structural properties of different architectural forms.

He was able to represent with extraordinary plastic clarity the structure of a spiral staircase in one of his schemes for a palace for the French king.

Exhibition design has been an important strand in Stanton Williams' work ever since the formation of the practice in 1985. The office has created spaces in a wide range of venues for more than 50 exhibitions, both temporary and permanent. Each commission inevitably presents its own challenges and solutions, requiring a balance to be struck between curatorial ambition, the demands of the objects being displayed, and the scope of the exhibition space itself. Nonetheless, certain common threads link the results, not least concern for lighting, scale, and the relationship of people to space—elements which are central to architecture.

Some exhibition venues have been conceived to be permanent. The Triforium Gallery at Winchester Cathedral, for example, creates space for the display of art and historical treasures within the eleventh century building. The Gas Hall, Birmingham, a Victorian structure, was transformed into an international standard flexible space for temporary exhibitions. Similarly adaptable in intent were new galleries created for London's Design Museum. Compton Verney, Warwickshire, offers a sequence of galleries that begins with the restored public rooms of the classical country house and moves via a series of abstracted areas in which old and new are juxtaposed to a wholly-new flexible gallery located within an addition to the original building.

Many more commissions, however, have involved the design of spaces for temporary exhibitions. Subjects have ranged from the historic to the contemporary: from Romanesque art, Leonardo da Vinci and Canaletto to Bridget Riley, Pop Art, and Gerhard Richter. These exhibitions have been staged in a wide range of venues: from the classical grandeur of the V&A Museum, Tate Britain, Royal Academy and the National Portrait Gallery, to the concrete 'Brutalism' of the South Bank's Hayward Gallery.

Seemingly diffuse at first glance, these projects are tied together by a number of themes. Collaboration is crucial in order to understand curators' ideas, artists' intentions, plus the needs, content and context of the objects themselves. Environmental and security factors inevitably play a significant role, from the scale of the whole gallery to the detailed design of a showcase. The possibilities and limitations of the exhibition venue must be considered. Over and above all this, however, the creation of successful space for display, whether permanent or temporary, is founded on the nature of the relationship between object and viewer and an understanding of the way in which people move through space. The scale and sequencing of display areas, the extent to which space is contained or released, as well as juxtapositions and the provision of glimpses between spaces all make important contributions to the experience of the exhibition. So too do the style and intensity of lighting (both natural and artificial), which can transform the mood, highlight objects, and draw people through the exhibition.

The results are something of a paradox: public spaces for private contemplation. They are, however, no less architecture than buildings in the conventional sense. Indeed, exhibition design can be understood as a particularly closely-focused architecture, in which space, light, materials and movement take on a heightened quality.

Staging a Thought
Ken Arnold

Exhibition curators forge ideas by experimenting with the connections between things and novel ideas in public places. They invariably ply their craft in three-dimensions, and a self-conscious awareness of the space of an exhibition is absolutely crucial to their effectiveness. For galleries do so much more than merely house shows. They add colour and character, of course; they decorate exhibition topics. But they are also embedded with their own messages, meanings and ideas, inevitably adding their own voice. Even without formal architectural or design training, curators need to pay careful attention to the nature of the floors, ceilings and walls of exhibition halls, to the lighting, to the plinths, text panels, labels and so forth. Professionally speaking, however, it tends to be designers who are responsible for the visual setting of a show. Consequently, as the art historian Martin Kemp points out, the moment when designers get involved in an exhibition has a strong bearing on the visitors' physical experiences of it. Kemp recommends their early involvement, rather than getting them "to design an exhibition which has (already) been conceived, ... (making sure the designer) is part of the conceptual framing of it".

Surprisingly maybe, the role of the designer in articulating the idea of an exhibition has received somewhat more analysis than that of the curator. A focus on the visitors' experiences led, from the 1930s onwards, to a particular concern with how effective communications could emerge from the collaborative effort of curators and designers in bonding the story and its look. As an example, historian Charlotte Klonk has shown how early twentieth century German designers (working both in museum and commercial settings) applied themselves to the task of engaging visitors first by visually attracting their attention, and then by providing a 'pleasant stroll', relating exhibits or objects one to another and imparting information with impact. The critic of the time, Karl Scheffler summed up the core understanding that enabled them to do this as "the fundamental laws of bodily feeling and (how to) articulate them in space".

Early analysis of the exhibition experience assumed the model of a passive audience being led along from one node of information to another. More recently, however, most museum researchers have instead adopted a different view in which visitors have become active participants in their own experiences, 'collaborating' with the exhibition makers in how the spaces are negotiated and how meaning is extracted from them. And as Martin Kemp insists, their self-constructed experience of the show starts at its threshold. Stanton Williams, Kemp's favoured exhibition designer, insists on providing an initial quiet space and perhaps a single object or some other element that enables visitors mentally to shake off the frustrations of getting to the venue: a decompression chamber of sorts in which they can gain composure and embrace the exhibition itself.

Once over this threshold and thoroughly within the exhibition, arguably the most important element of designing/curating the visitor experience lies in the art of juxtaposition—that is in creating the gaps and pauses that articulate the physical and mental passage between one thing and another. Though blindingly obvious, it is crucial to remember that this experience of moving on is fundamentally ambulatory, albeit in the rather unusual conditions of relative darkness and at an artificially slow pace. This 'museum walk'—the tryingly controlled, cleric-like movement that visitors have to make with their feet or wheelchair wheels in order to get round an exhibition—provides the governing pace and pattern of their mental meanderings. Focusing on walking as a fundamentally cerebral experience is the great insight that Rebecca Solnit shares in her *Wanderlust: a history of walking.* The history of walking, she insists, has also to be understood as a history of thinking. And from the eighteenth century on, she argues, when the idea of controlling, taming and moulding the environment in order to "stage a thought" first emerged, walking became an important part of the history of ideas—a form of constructed visual journey for the imagination, "leisurely enough both to see and to think over the sights, to assimilate the new into the known". And while walking "everything stays connected". To walk, Solnit further asserts, is to put the mind in motion at about three miles per hour. Exhibitions, it seems to me, provide a special, and especially concentrated, form of this mental movement, where the speed is dramatically slowed down to maybe closer to 0.3 miles per hour. This is the pace of an average visitors' stuttering progress and thought processes through a show: their "investigations, rituals and meditations". Fundamentally then, the job of the exhibition team is to choreograph a gripping stroll through one or more medium-sized rooms.

In practice, this concept of curatorship as an exercise in controlling the chance visual encounters of a stroller (ensuring that they have an interesting walk) was already central to early exhibition experiments by, for example, Bauhaus artist Lázló Moholy-Nagy. His 1929 display in Zehlendorf (a Berlin suburb) employed the careful placing of doors, walls and corridors, so that, as Charlotte Klonk describes it, "the visitor (had) the feeling of a leisurely walk without losing the aim or the security of an aim from consciousness". This rigorous and rational approach to ordering a visitor's experience of an exhibition (as some sort of architectural performance) was described by Adolf Behne at the time as "an organised path along a specific set of objects in a specific unequivocal direction and sequence". This tightly choreographed approach to exhibition making, which arguably can be traced back to Renaissance masques and before, continues today in, for example, parts of David Wilson's Museum of Jurassic Technology in Los Angeles and in the highly cinematographic exhibitions of filmmaker Peter Greenaway, as well as in some rather old-fashioned didactic science exhibitions. But even here, visitors are able to exercise their own inclinations for free association and meaning-making. For all that, though the passage through the space might be overtly led and the preferred sequence of stimuli suggestively implied, the exhibits themselves, the fashion in which they are examined, and the stories embodied within them nevertheless remain irrepressibly open.

IN THE END, IT'S ALL ABOUT THIS

In the end, it's all about this
Stephen Bayley

"In the end, it's all about this"

Paul Williams said it over lunch when theatrically passing me a fine white Rosenthal bowl of extra virgin olive oil. The setting was Stanton Williams' London studio where I was having lunch with him and Alan Stanton. The studio being a good metaphor of their approach to architecture as any literary conceit I can concoct, at least for the time being.

Invisible from the street, it has an understated—indeed, apparently, underground—presence even after you have passed the threshold of the larger complex it occupies. But it is a sort of understatement that is full of confident emphasis and quiet consideration. Good manners are more likely the result of well-earned self-possession rather than timorousness.

So the offer of the olive oil was, while gratefully received, not just *politesse*, more an illustration of what architecture should do. Which is to say make available a congenial experience. I am often asked what makes a good building and after years of agonising about it, with futile and embarrassing philosophical diversions, I now know the answer. If it makes you feel good, then it passes the test. For all its apparent simplicity, the Stanton Williams studio is quietly powerful in effect: the simplicity is hard-won, as simplicity always is. Any fool can make things complicated. And the site, at first, almost an apologetic demurral, turns out to be a stunning canal-side location, steely with radiant light even on a dull day. The great thing about subtlety is that it reaches a more fundamental part of the psyche than extravagance or flamboyance.

But I like using literary equivalents in architectural criticism. Pastiche and doggerel, for example, are rarely exalting either in books or buildings. On the other hand, the best buildings have a narrative structure, like a novel, rather as the Stanton Williams office only reveals itself as you work your way through it. You cannot, perhaps, tell a building by its cover. You have to read it all the way to the end.

To continue the metaphor, some buildings might even have a plot. Others are farcical, dramatic. Possibly even tragic. And I am certain that exhibition design is the architectural equivalent of a short story. It's a short-form narrative. All the elements of a novel—character, narrative, plot—are in miniature. This means they have to be even more carefully considered. Often considered a poor relation of architecture, I prefer to see exhibitions as a discipline at least as exacting. Anyway, let's not forget that Paxton's 1851 Crystal Palace and Mies' 1929 Barcelona Pavilion and even Sir Leslie Martin's 1951 Royal Festival Hall were, in any case, buildings at an exhibition.

It was with exhibition design that, quite inadvertently, I became one of Stanton Williams' very first clients. The context was the V&A. Here, the very same day in 1974 that Roy Strong walked in through the front door, Paul Williams came in through the goods entrance around the back via the mysteriously named Science Gate. Williams is a rare example of a first division architect who initially trained as a designer. And what a very odd reflection of the narcissistic preoccupations of the architectural profession that is.

When Paul Williams joined the V&A in London 1974, Alan Stanton was still working on the Centre Pompidou, another great exhibition building. He was, among other things, trying to convince Pontus Hulten to develop a system of floating screens for the new Museum of Modern Art. It's significant, I think, that while Williams was at the V&A with Roy Strong, Stanton was in Paris with Pontus Hulten. Roy Strong has many critics, but I am not one of them. Strong helped make the sleepy V&A into a part of national life with a series of exhibitions, some of which Williams designed, that recognised the purpose of a museum was to campaign and entertain, as well as instruct. Hulten, according to Niki de Saint-Phalle, had "the soul of an artist, not a museum director". Certainly, he radicalised the idea of what an exhibition might be. His *She—a cathedral of 1966* in Stockholm's Moderna Museet had visitors entering between the legs of a giant woman. His 1968 *The Machine Seen at the End of the Mechanical Age* in New York's Museum of Modern Art was, with a catalogue bound in stamped and printed metal, a bravura exercise in post-Pop.

I see influences of this background in Stanton Williams' work. Together, of course, with Carlo Scarpa whose impressive shadow it is impossible for any exhibition designer to avoid. But stylish as these individuals most certainly were, exhibition design is, of course, not just a matter of style. The functional requirements are exacting: visitors engage with objects and images with an intensity magnified because it is of short duration. They explained to me once that as soon as you get closer to a wall than your own height, the relationship with it becomes very different. This is just one way that exhibitions require their designers to make decisions about space and proportions, about intimacy and awkwardness.

Every conversation I have had with Paul Williams and Alan Stanton returns to three themes. The first is their neo-dogmatic refusal to theorise ("The buildings should speak for themselves"). The second is the proper understanding of materials and details. The third is what, if you were going in for literary conceits, you might call the Zen of ordinary things. Actually, I say these are three themes, but in fact it is one. And this is the absolute insistence on visual discipline.

But first, the theory thing. Of course, to claim to have no theory is a theory in itself. "We've never wanted to be a part of any school" they say, nearly in chorus. In our deliciously complicated world there is no such thing as a value-free decision to be neutral: rather as going around naked is not a denial of the importance of clothes, but a stirring testament to their profound significance. Still, when they insist they have a "feel for stuff" you can sense two things.

First, their background in the Midlands where it was impossible to be brought up and not be aware of manufacturing and all the different disciplines and skills and, indeed, art that goes into shaping metal. Second, in this statement too there is a ghostly echo of the Bauhaus and its ideas of learning-by-doing. Bauhaus teachers, including Benno Zehnder, found a refuge in the Birmingham College of Art where Williams was taught.

And when they say that they miss working directly with material, contact with lathes, metalwork and files, that's not mere nostalgia (not that there is anything "mere" about this powerful emotion), but something rather like a credo. When they say "Listen to the equipment. You know by the sound if it's working well" that's a matter-of-fact interpretation of the Machine Aesthetic. This sounds almost like a theory to me.

For such a calm and controlled pair, the matter of materials and details stirs deeply submerged oceanic currents of emotion. "It's a painful existence being visual. Just walking down the street...." And then the thought dies in a recollection of the clutter and mess of the world outside. Stanton and Williams may not want to be associated with any school, but they are absolutely at one with *l'esprit moderne* which, I am coming to think, can best be defined as a passionate need to tidy-up. "We always want to model absolutely everything on a project—sometimes at full size, in order to really understand and to get a feel for the spaces and the details", Stanton explained. I doubt that Paul Williams was exaggerating when he told me "I know every nut and bolt of the Millennium Seed Bank", but this mechanical attention to detail is complicated by fastidious artistry. Williams explained that he often found the engineers had a single-path solution to a particular problem of, say, a fixing. Fair enough, but for Stanton Williams a purely functional solution is not quite enough. That fixing has got to have the "visually correct" weight and thickness.

So, to the Zen of ordinary things. But first, three curious insights into this most committed and dedicated pair whose apparent austerity, in fact, belies more colourful and emotional activity. One. Besides Carlo Scarpa what, gentlemen, are your influences? Louis Kahn for his magisterial treatment of space. More surprisingly, Luis Barragan for his commitment to magic and beauty. Two. These Eames chairs, I asked, aren't they really antiques? No doubt about the answer: "Yes they are!" Three. Why, have you not built houses for yourselves?: "You mean 'yet'?"

So I think this means Stanton Williams are committed to the pleasure principle. It also means they see no reason why past and present need be separate in their office or in their work, as they demonstrate so very well at, for example, Whitby and Compton Verney. Last, there really is no hurry. Good ideas, even if you have no theory, are self-dependent powers which, as Goldsmith had it, "can time defy as rocks resist the billows and the sky".

Which, for the very last time, brings us back to Zen. When Alan Stanton and Paul Williams were students, Eugen Herrigel's counter-culture classic *Zen and the Art of Archery* (US edition 1953) was still in libraries and bookshops. Herrigel was, perhaps, a bit of a fraud, but his little book caught the mood of a generation. In it we can read "The archer ceases to be conscious of himself as the one who is engaged in hitting the bull's eye. This state of unconsciousness is realised only when, completely empty and rid of the self, he becomes at one with the projecting of his technical skill."

Herrigel's book created a tradition. In 1974 Robert Pirsig published *Zen and the Art of Motorcycle Maintenance* a fictionalised account of a seventeen day ride across America which gave rise, among many other remarkable things, to *The Times Literary Supplement* using a cut-away drawing of a 750 Kawasaki on its normally stuffy cover. Pirsig's aim was to show how, given the right attitude, even the most banal things (changing sump oil or replacing a damaged shock-absorber, for instance) might become nearly mystical experiences. So, a shogun's archery lesson might influence the design of a transom.

I mentioned this to them just after Paul had passed me the olive oil. I said what it's all about, if you ask me, it is the ordinary thing made extraordinary. They lit up. "The ordinary thing made extraordinary! That's exactly what we would like people to say about our work." So I have.

WORKS

1986

The RIBA Architecture Centre
(project) London
Client: Royal Institute
of British Architects

National Portrait Gallery—new wing
(project) London
Client: The National Portrait Gallery

1988

Masson (exhibition)
Hayward Gallery, London
Client: Southbank Centre

Diego Rivera (exhibition)
Hayward Gallery, London
Client: Southbank Centre

Rodin (exhibition)
Hayward Gallery, London
Client: Southbank Centre

The Age of Chivalry (exhibition)
Royal Academy, London
Client: Royal Academy of Arts

St Mary Abbots Housing
(project) London
Client: Private

Roger Fenton (exhibition)
Hayward Gallery, London
Client: Southbank Centre

**Angry Penguins and Realist
Painting in Melbourne in the 1940s**
(exhibition)
Hayward Gallery, London
Client: Southbank Centre

**Master Paintings from
The Phillips Collection** (exhibition)
Hayward Gallery, London
Client: Southbank Centre

Lucian Freud (exhibition)
Hayward Gallery, London
Client: Southbank Centre

1990

The Design Museum Galleries
London
Client: Design Museum

Tate St Ives Gallery
(competition) Cornwall
Client: Tate Gallery

French Design (exhibition)
Design Museum, London
Client: Design Museum

Art in Latin America (exhibition)
Hayward Gallery, London
Client: Southbank Centre

**The Other Story: Afro-Asian artists
in post-war Britain** (exhibition)
Hayward Gallery, London
Client: Southbank Centre

Issey Miyake: Women
London
Client: Issey Miyake International

Coca Cola—Boiler House Gallery
Victoria & Albert Museum, London
Client: Victoria & Albert Museum

The Boyle Family (exhibition)
Hayward Gallery, London
Client: Southbank Centre

L'Amour Fou: Photography and Surrealism (exhibition)
Hayward Gallery, London
Client: Southbank Centre

Dreams of a Summer Night: Scandinavian Painting (exhibition)
Hayward Gallery, London
Client: Southbank Centre

Falls the Shadow: Recent British and European Art (exhibition) Hayward Gallery, London
Client: Arts Council of Great Britain

Issey Miyake: Men
London
Client: Issey Miyake International

1989

The Tiger Rugs of Tibet (exhibition)
Hayward Gallery, London
Client: Southbank Centre

Nam June Paik (exhibition)
Hayward Gallery, London
Client: Southbank Centre

St George-in-the-East
(project) London
Client: St George-in-the-East Trust

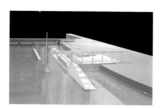

The Chinese Scroll (exhibition)
Hayward Gallery, London
Client: Southbank Centre

RFAC Thames Study
(project) London
Client: Royal Fine Arts Society

Twilight of the Tsars: Jasper Johns (exhibition)
Hayward Gallery, London
Client: Southbank Centre

1990

Bolder Bridge House
(project) Hampshire
Client: Private

The British Art Show (exhibition)
Hayward Gallery, London
Client: Southbank Centre

Magnum (exhibition)
Hayward Gallery, London
Client: Southbank Centre

American Graphics (exhibition)
Hayward Gallery, London
Client: Southbank Centre

Winogrand (exhibition)
Hayward Gallery, London
Client: Southbank Centre

**Russian Art at the Turn of
the Century** (exhibition)
Hayward Gallery, London
Client: Southbank Centre

1991

Whistles: Fenwicks
London
Client: Whistles

The British Art Show
(exhibition) Glasgow
Client: McClennan Gallery

Whistles: St Christopher Place
London
Client: Whistles

1992

Kriston Laundry
London
Client: Kriston

RIBA: Reception Room Gallery
London
Client: Royal Institute
of British Architects

Hayward Gallery: Shop
London
Client: Southbank Centre

Toulouse-Lautrec (exhibition)
Hayward Gallery, London
Client: Southbank Centre

Double Take (exhibition)
Hayward Gallery, London
Client: Southbank Centre

Munakata (exhibition)
Hayward Gallery
Client: Southbank Centre

Magritte (exhibition)
Hayward Gallery, London
Client: Southbank Centre

Ancient Art of Mexico (exhibition)
Hayward Gallery, London
Client: Southbank Centre

1993

Classic FM studio/offices
London
Client: Classic FM

Visitor Centre (competition)
Wakehurst Place, West Sussex
Client: Royal Botanic Gardens Kew

Art of Process (exhibition)
RIBA, London
Client: Royal Institute
of British Architects

Bridget Riley (exhibition)
Hayward Gallery, London
Client: Southbank Centre

Artists Studio
London
Client: Val Archer

Osho Gallery
London
Client: Osho International

Metropolis—Tokyo Design Vision
(exhibition) London
Client: Design Museum

**Issey Miyake: Plantation/
apartment/office**
London
Client: Issey Miyake International

**The Triforium Gallery
Winchester Cathedral** Hampshire
Client: The Dean and Chapter
of Winchester Cathedral

Stanton Williams (exhibition)
London
Client: Royal Institute
of British Architects

The Gas Hall Gallery
Birmingham
Client: City of Birmingham
Museum & Art Gallery

German Romanticism (exhibition)
Hayward Gallery, London
Client: Southbank Centre

1993

Africa Centre
(project) London
Client: The Africa Centre

Georgia O'Keefe (exhibition)
Hayward Gallery, London
Client: Southbank Centre

Aratjara (exhibition)
Hayward Gallery, London
Client: Southbank Centre

Canaletto & England (exhibition)
Birmingham Gas Hall
Client: City of Birmingham
Museum & Art Gallery

Old Royal Observatory Galleries
London
Client: National Maritime Museum

Roger Hilton (exhibition)
Hayward Gallery, London
Client: Southbank Centre

Salvador Dali: The Early Years
(exhibition)
Hayward Gallery, London
Client: Southbank Centre

Possibilities in Painting (exhibition)
Hayward Gallery, London
Client: Southbank Centre

1994

60 Sloane Avenue Building
London
Client: Baylight/John Mattson
AB Fastighets

Yves Klein (exhibition)
Hayward Gallery, London
Client: Southbank Centre

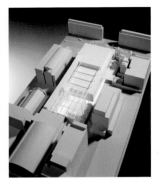

Science Museum—new wing
(competition) London
Client: The Science Museum

French Landscapes (exhibition)
Hayward Gallery, London
Client: Southbank Centre

Royal William Yard Bridge
(competition) Plymouth
Client: Royal William Yard

1996

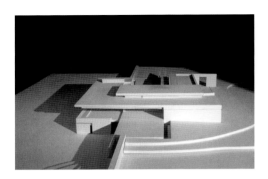

Mere Farm House
(project) Wiltshire
Private Client

Mica House—Penthouse
London
Private Client

University of Brighton—School of Art
(project) East Sussex
Client: University of Brighton

**National Maritime Museum,
Queens House**
(project) London
Client: National Maritime Museum

Gateshead Music Centre
(competition) Gateshead
Client: Gateshead Development
Corporation

Hackney Empire
(competition) London
Client: Hackney Empire

St Mary's Mansions—Apartment
London
Private Client

Soros Gallery (project)
Kiev, Ukraine
Client: Soros Foundation

Bonnard (exhibition)
Hayward Gallery, London
Client: Southbank Centre

900 Years: The Restoration of
Westminster Abbey (exhibition)
St Margaret's Church, London
Client: Westminster Abbey

Field Study Centre
Wakehurst Place, West Sussex
Client: Royal Botanic Gardens Kew

Pyx Chamber
Westminster Abbey, London
Client: Dean and Chapter
of Westminster Abbey

Clore Management Centre
Birkbeck College, London
Client: University of London

Issey Miyake: Pleats Please
Brook Street, London
Client: Issey Miyake International

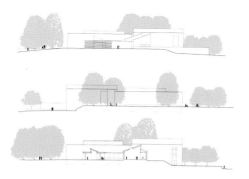

JF Willumsens Museum
(competition) Denmark
Client: Byggedirektoratet

Royal National Theatre—
masterplan and modernisation
London
Client: RNT Board

Metro Studio Complex
London
Client: Metro Imaging

Ashmolean Museum—extension
Oxford
Client: University of Oxford

Compton Verney Art Gallery
Warwickshire
Client: Compton Verney
House Trust

Stanton Williams (exhibition)
Royal National Theatre, London
Client: Stanton Williams

Birkbeck College: Additions
(project) London
Client: University of London

Museum of Modern Art Masterplan
Oxford
Client: Museum of Modern Art

National Gallery: Central Hall
(project)
National Gallery, London
Client: National Gallery

Henrietta Street Apartment
London
Private Client

4 Brindleyplace
Birmingham
Client: Argent Group

Spectacular Bodies (exhibition)
Hayward Gallery, London
Client: Southbank Centre

Dyson Gallery: Phase II
London
Client: Design Museum

Royal Geographical Society
(competition) London
Client: Royal Geographical Society

Museum of London
(competition) London
Client: Museum of London

The Art of Bloomsbury (exhibition)
Tate Gallery, London
Client: Tate Gallery

BBC Langham Place
(competition) London
Client: BBC

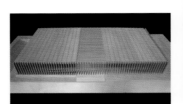

Castle Ashby Conference Centre
(project) Northamptonshire
Client: Castle Ashby

Casa Fontana
Lugano, Switzerland
Client: Private

1999

Hounmere House
(project) Surrey
Client: Private

Issey Miyake: Conduit Street
London
Client: Issey Miyake International

2000

Piccadilly Gardens
(competition) Manchester
Client: Argent

Wellcome Trust Millennium Bulding
Wakehurst Place, West Sussex
Client: The Royal Botanic
Gardens Kew

Transit of the Body Exhibition
(competition) Barcelona, Spain
Client: Edifici la Marina Seca

2001

Place Cornavin (project)
Geneva, Switzerland
Client: Ville de Genève

Royal College of Music
(competition) London
Client: Royal College of Music

Turin Cultural Centre
(competition) Italy
Client: Comune di Torino

Museum of Kenya
(project) Nairobi, Kenya
Client: Museum of Kenya

Place des Alpes (competition)
Geneva, Switzerland
Client: Ville de Genève

2001

The Panopticon Building
(competition) London
Client: University College London

Hampton Court Palace Fountain
(competition) Surrey
Client: Historic Royal Palaces

**Central St Martins College:
Holborn** (project) London
Client: London Institute

2002

RCA: Sculpture Building
(competition) London
Client: Royal College of Art

Selfridges: Manchester Central
Manchester
Client: Selfridges & Co

Selfridges: Birmingham 2nd floor
Birmingham
Client: Selfridges & Co

Poulton Gorse House
(project) Gloucestershire
Client: Private

2003

Middlesbrough Town Hall
(competition) Middlesbrough
Client: Middlesbrough Council

Reading Town Centre
(competition) Reading
Client: AMEC/Borough of Reading

Florence Nightingale Museum
(competition) London
Client: Guys & St. Thomas' Hospital

Royal Ascot Hall of Fame
(project) Berkshire
Client: Turnberry Consulting

National Film and Television School
(project) London
Client: NFTS

Aston Hall/ Visitor Centre
(project) Birmingham
Client: Birmingham Museum
& Art Gallery

Paul Klee (exhibition)
Hayward Gallery, London
Client: Southbank Centre

Issey Miyake: Pleats Please
Kings Road, London
Client: Issey Miyake International

Charles Darwin Centre
(competition) Bromley, Kent
Client: AEA Consulting

Paddington Basin
(competition) London
Client: Derwent

Constable (exhibition)
Grand Palais, Paris
Client: British Council

Whitby Abbey Headland Project
Yorkshire
Client: Engllish Heritage

Bridget Riley (exhibition)
Tate Britain, London
Client: Tate Britain

Royal Albert Memorial Museum
(competition) Exeter
Client: Exeter City Council

South London Gallery
(project) London
Client: South London Gallery

Cadbury: Bournville Masterplan
Birmingham
Client: Cadbury Trebor Bassett

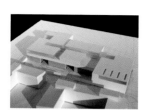

University of Hertfordshire:
Feasibility Study
Hertfordshire
Client: University of Hertfordshire

Selfridges: Oxford Street
First and second floors
London
Client: Selfridges & Co

This Was Tomorrow (exhibition)
Tate Britain, London
Client: Tate Britain

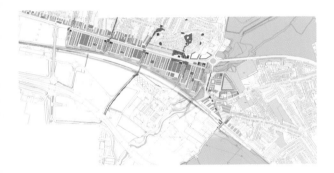

Rainham: Urban Design Framework
London
Client: London Borough of Havering

Redchurch Street Apartments
(project) London
Client: Private

**Central St Martins College:
Charing Cross Road**
London
Client: University of the Arts London

Monsoon Kings Road
(project) London
Client: Mountgrange

Sandwell College (competition)
West Midlands
Client: Sandwell College

V&A Renaissance Gallery
(competition) London
Client: Victoria & Albert Museum

Royal Academy Restaurant
(competition) London
Client: Royal Academy of Arts

Tower Hill
Tower of London
Client: Historic Royal Palaces

Compton Verney: Phase II
Warwickshire
Client: Compton Verney
House Trust

Nottingham Bottle Lane
(competition) Nottinghamshire
Client: Bildburn Properties

**City University: School of
Social Sciences**
London
Client: City University

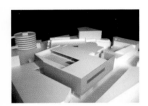

M&S Store Newcastle
(project) Newcastle
Client: Marks & Spencer

RSA Masterplan
London
Client: Royal Society of Arts

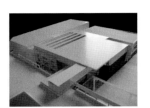

M&S Store Plymouth: Masterplan
Plymouth
Client: Marks & Spencer

M&S Store Norwich: Masterplan
Norwich
Client: Marks & Spencer

Central St Martins College: Backhill
London
Client: University of the Arts London

Lowther Castle
(competition) Cumbria
Client: Trustees of the Lowther
Castle and Gardens Trust

A4 Green Corridor
(competition) London
Client: GLA

Acton Masterplan
(competition) London
Client: London Borough of Ealing

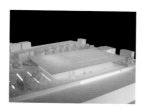

Chester University Performing Arts
(competition) Cheshire
Client: Chester University

Tate St Ives extension
(competition) Cornwall
Client: Tate Gallery

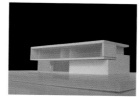

Kenilworth Castle
(competition) Warwickshire
Client: English Heritage

Millfield School Pavilion
(project) Street, Somerset
Client: Millfield School

Crossness Pumping Station
(competition) London
Client: Crossness Engines Trust

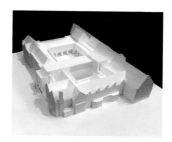

Sloane Square
(project) London
Client: Royal Borough of
Kensington & Chelsea

King Edward VI Grammar School
(project) Chelmsford, Essex
Client: King Edward VI
Grammar School

2004

Warwick Museum
(project) Warwickshire
Client: Warwickshire
County Council

**Barking Town Centre Urban
Design Proposal**
(competition) London
Client: London Borough of
Barking & Dagenham

Ruthin Craft Centre
(competition) Denbighshire
Client: The Arts Council of Wales

Turnberry Consulting Offices
London
Client: Turnberry Consulting

M&S Store Dundrum (project)
Dundrum, Ireland
Client: Marks & Spencer

2005

Cranfield University: Masterplan
Bedfordshire
Client: Cranfield University

Wimpey Rainham housing
(project) London
Client: Taylor Wimpey UK

M&S Store Bristol
(project) Bristol
Client: Marks & Spencer

New Cross Gate: Consultancy
London
Client: London Borough
of Lewisham

Wartski Jewellery Store
(project) London
Client: Wartski

Mary Rose Museum
(competition) Portsmouth
Client: The Mary Rose Trust

Woodberry Down
(competition) London
Client: Southern Housing Group

2006

Hull History Centre
(competition) Hull
Client: Hull City Council

Royal Shakespeare Company
(competition)
Stratford-upon-Avon
Client: Royal Shakespeare
Company

Wolvercote Paper Mill
(competition) Oxfordshire
Client: University of Oxford

King's College Strand Campus
(competition) London
Client: King's College London.

St Paul's School (competition)
London
Client: St Paul's School

St Martin's Walk Redevelopment
(project) Dorking
Client: Thornfield Properties

Clove Building: Fit-out
London
Client: Dorrington Properties

King's Cross Urban Realm
(competition) London
Client: London Borough
of Camden

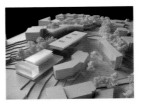

**Bournemouth Winter Gardens
Development**
(competition) Dorset
Client: Bournemouth Council

Portsmouth Department Store
(competition) Portsmouth
Client: Centros Miller

2007

Leonardo da Vinci (exhibition)
V&A Museum, London
Client: Victoria & Albert Museum

The Warren, Woolwich
(project) London
Client: Berkeley Homes

The Peak Resort
Chesterfield, Derbyshire
Client: Birchall Properties

First Emperor Exhibition
(competition)
British Museum, London
Client: British Museum

V&A Jewellery Gallery
(competition)
V&A Museum, London
Client: Victoria & Albert Museum

Truro Cathedral Precinct
(project) Cornwall
Client: Truro Cathedral

Wembley—Transport/Masterplan
London
Client: London Borough of Brent

Golden Square Offices
(project) London
Client: Baylight Properties

Argenta House Apartments
(project) London
Client: Findon Holdings

Pop Art Portraits (exhibition)
National Portrait Gallery, London
Client: National Portrait Gallery

**Seduced: Art & Sex from
Antiquity to Now** (exhibition)
Barbican Gallery, London
Client: Barbican Centre

Centre for Creative Arts, Bath
(competition) Somerset
Client: University of Bath

Belgrade Theatre
Coventry
Client: Belgrade Theatre Trust

2007

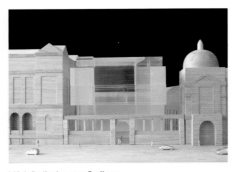

V&A Boilerhouse Gallery
Feasibility Study
London
Client: Victoria & Albert Museum

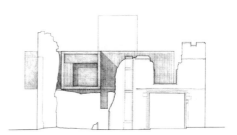

Astley Castle (competition)
Nuneaton, Warwickshire
Client: The Landmark Trust

2008

Beethoven Development,
(competition) Netherlands
Client: ING Real Estate
Development

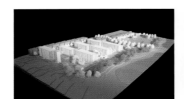

Warwick University—Student
Accommodation
(competition) Warwickshire
Client: Warwick University

Cadbury: Bournville Place
Birmingham
Client: Cadbury

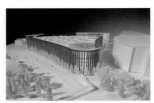

Preston Tithebarn Car Park
(competition) Lancashire
Client: Lend Lease

Elizabeth House
(competition) Manchester
Client: Argent Group

Stringfellow Hall—
Student Accommodation
Bedfordshire
Client: Cranfield University

Clark's Shoe Museum
(competition) Street, Somerset
Client: Alfred Gillett Trust
for C&J Clark Limited

Byam Shaw Art College
London
Client: University of Arts London

Hackney Central Station
(competition)
London
Client: Transport for London

Shah Abbas Exhibition
(competition) London
Client: British Museum

Crawley New Town Hall
Sussex
Client: Crawley Borough Council

Waterloo Road Hotel
London
Client: Ebury Securities

Clove Building: Extension
London
Client: Dorrington Properties

The British Museum Collections
(competition)
British Museum, London
Client: British Museum

Riverwalk House
London
Client: Derwent London

St Clare House: Fit-out
London
Client: Dorrington Properties

Department Store
Bristol
Client: Bristol Alliance (Hammerson)

**Royal Tunbridge Wells
Cinema Site**
(competition) Kent
Client: Lordland Europe

Königswinter: Drachenfelsplateau
(competition) Germany
Client: Stadt Königswinter

2009

Gerhard Richter Portraits
(exhibition)
National Portrait Gallery, London
Client: National Portrait Gallery

V&A Ceramics Galleries
V&A Museum, London
Client: Victoria & Albert Museum

Brunel University Space Study
Uxbridge, Middlesex
Client: Brunel University

Fitzroy Park House
London
Client: Private

Padova Botanic Gardens
Italy
Client: Università' di Padova

Hackney Marshes Community Hub
London
Client: London Borough of Hackney

Bourne Hill Offices
Salisbury
Client: Wiltshire Council

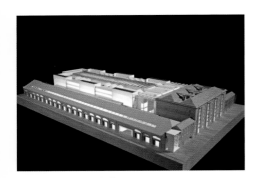

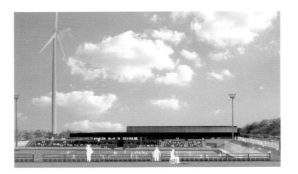

**Central St Martins College:
King's Cross**
London
Client: University of the Arts London

London 2012 Olympics: Eton Manor
London
Client: Olympic Delivery Authority

Sainsbury Laboratory
Cambridge
Client: University of Cambridge
& Gatsby Charitable Foundation

King's Cross Pavilion
London
Client: Argent Group

Stadtmuseum Berlin
Germany
Client: Senatsverwaltung für
Stadtentwicklung

Garden Building: Extension
Lincoln College, Oxford
Client: Lincoln College,
University Of Oxford

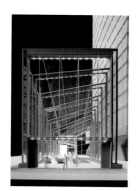

Centrepoint Plaza
London
Client: London Underground/
Transport for London/LB Camden

Tower Hill Gateway Interchange
London
Client: Transport for London

Turner and The Masters (exhibition)
Tate Britain, London
Client: Tate Gallery

Britten–Pears Archive Building
Aldeburgh, Suffolk
Client: Britten Pears Foundation

**Bexhill-on-Sea Seafront
Improvement Scheme**
East Sussex
Client: Rother District Council

**Chilver Hall—Student
Accommodation**
Bedfordshire
Client: Cranfield University

**Central St Martins College:
King's Cross Fit-out**
London
Client: University of Arts London

Directors and Associates

Alan Stanton
AA Dip(Hons) MArch RIBA RSA RDI

After studying at the Architectural Association in London, Alan worked briefly with Norman Foster before moving to California to study at UCLA, where he was awarded a fellowship in Urban Design. During his time in California he co-founded Chrysalis with a group of architects and artists. Returning to Europe, Alan worked with Renzo Piano and Richard Rogers on the Centre Pompidou in Paris. Following its completion he taught at the Architectural Association and established his own practice working on projects in the UK, France and Italy.

Alan formed the partnership with Paul Williams in 1985. As founding directors they have been responsible for the creative direction of the practice since its inception, and continue to have a leading design role in the studio's projects.

Alan has been Vice President of the Architectural Association Council, and a member of CABE design review panel and the RIBA Awards Committee. He has lectured extensively in this country and abroad, and has acted as external examiner at the Architectural Association, Kingston University, University of East London, Oxford Brookes University and Glasgow School of Art.

Alan became a Royal Designer for Industry in 2005 and is currently an external examiner at Greenwich University.

Paul Williams
BA H DiplAD RIBA RSA RDI

After graduating from Birmingham College of Art, Paul worked in the Design Studio at the Victoria & Albert Museum, London. While at the V&A he was awarded a research grant to study museum and gallery design at Yale. On his return from America, he headed the design studio for a further two years before establishing his own London-based practice in 1979, designing permanent gallery installations and art exhibitions internationally.

Paul formed the partnership with Alan Stanton in 1985. As founding directors they have been responsible for the creative direction of the practice since its inception, and continue to have a leading design role in the studio's projects.

In 2002, Paul was elected an Honorary Fellow of the RIBA. Later in the same year, he became the first British design trained practitioner architect to be registered by ARB (Architects Registration Board) and gain membership of the RIBA.

His former roles include Trustee of the Whitechapel Art Gallery, Architectural Advisor to the Heritage Lottery Fund and CABE, and chair of RIBA Regional Awards Panel. He has lectured extensively in this country and abroad, and has acted as external examiner at the Universities of Westminster, Plymouth, and Dundee and currently at Birmingham University.

Paul became a Royal Designer for Industry in 2005 and is presently a member of Architectural Advisory Panels to the Royal Borough of Kensington and Chelsea, and St Paul's Cathedral.

Gavin Henderson
MA (CANTAB) Dip Arch RIBA

Gavin graduated from Cambridge and Harvard. He was awarded the RIBA Bronze medal for his undergraduate work, and gained a commendation for the RIBA Silver Medal for postgraduate work. After graduating he worked for Eric Parry Architects where he was involved in a project to transform the Chateau du Paulin in Tarn, France.

Gavin joined Stanton Williams in 1994 and has been involved in a number of high profile and award winning projects including the Millennium Seedbank at Wakehurst Place, Sussex, Compton Verney Art Gallery in Warwickshire, and proposals for Sloane Square, London.

Gavin is currently leading the new Sainsbury Laboratory for the University of Cambridge and the Stadtmuseum in Berlin.

Gavin has taught in architecture studios at the University of North London and has been a visiting critic/ lecturer at various UK universities.

Peter Murray
Dip Arch RIBA

Peter studied architecture at Melbourne University and the Polytechnic of Central London, before working as an associate at two design practices, Dunthorne Parker Architects and Powell-Tuck Associates.

Peter joined Stanton Williams in 1990 and was involved in a number of Stanton Williams' earlier major projects, including Sloane Avenue, Ashmolean Museum, Compton Verney Art Gallery and Tower Hill at the Tower of London.

Peter now has a broader role in managing the practice and a key advice and mentoring responsibility across all projects in the studio. His wealth of architectural and management experience is incorporated into the project management and business procedures that he has developed for the practice.

Patrick Richard
Dip Arch EPFL SIA RIBA

Patrick studied at the Ecole Polytechnique Fédérale de Lausanne in Switzerland under Professor Luigi Snozzi. During his studies, Patrick worked for architect Zaha Hadid in London. After graduating, he worked in Switzerland, then established his own practice in France working on the transformation of an historic Abbey, winning a major commission for masterplanning the town of Pomier in Beaujolais and shortlisted for a masterplanning study in the city of Grenoble.

Patrick joined Stanton Williams in 1995 and has been involved in a number of high profile and award winning projects including the Casa Fontana house in Lugano, Switzerland, Four Brindleyplace in Birmingham, and the department store for House of Fraser in Bristol.

Patrick is currently leading several projects including student accommodation at Cranfield University, the redevelopment of Centre Point Plaza, London, and sports facilities at Hackney Marshes, London.

Patrick has acted as a visiting critic at Westminster, Kingston, Central Saint Martins and Brighton Universities and has lectured in the UK and France.

Associates
Doriano Chiarparin
Kalpesh Intwala
Kaori Ohsugi
Rawden Pettitt
Juliet Phillips
Richard Wardle

Roisin Aherne
Miraz Ahmed
Ram Ahronov
Caroline Aisida
Joanna Ako
Ann Armstrong
Adam Arts
Andre Baugh
Francesca Bergamini
Besnik Bijo
Oliver Bindloss
Brian Bishop
Simon Blunden
Robert Bochel
Stuart Bourne
Tim Brenan
Alex Buckland
Alexis Burrus
Alan Bushby
Andrea Castanheira
Gioia Castiglione
Kulbir Chada
Doriano Chiarparin
Yoon Choi
Chris Churchman
Monica Clarke
Emma Clayton
Simon Coley
Alistair Cook
Siew-Ching Cottis
Juliet Davis
Dusan Decermic
Madeleine Dignam
Philippa Ditcham
Bertil Donker
Kathryn Dunk
Charles Dymond
Heide van Eeden
Alan Farlie
David Farlie
Claudia Faust
Anne Fehrenbach
Mark Feighery
Bernado Figueirinhas
Tom Finch
Geraldine Flashman
Joanna Flint-Davies
Mary Arnold-Forster
Olivier Frayssineau
Kristian Garrecht
Francesco Garrutti
Andy Garton
Elena Gaydar
Jason Geen
Russell Gilchrist
Graham Gilmore
Sanjay Godhke
Amos Goldreich
Rebekah Gomez
Michael Greville
Richard Griffin
Jason Griffiths
Tom Gristwood
Robert Grover
Annakaisa Haanpaa
Stephen Hadley
Dorle Hahne
John Hatton

Jackie Hawke
Frank Heaversdege
Gavin Henderson
Anna Hesketh
Florian Holbe
Colin Holden
Gesa Hopkinson
Jane Houghton
David Hunter-Wade
Kalpesh Intwala
Simon Jandrup
Larissa Johnston
David Kahn
Inna Karmovytska
William Kavanagh
Delia Keane
Elke Kleindienst
Meretha Kristensen
Deborah Kuypers
Roo Lam Lau
Mike Langley
Nina Langner
Robert Letts
Amy Lindsay
Nicola Llowarch
Henrik Lønberg
Ana Lopes
Briony Lumb
Sally Mackereth
Rochelle Mahon
Ivan Margolius
Gary Marinko
Christopher Mascall
Jane Maskell
Simon McCormack
Alison McLellan
Aidan McMahon
Melissa Merryweather
Jerome Michel
Cathy Milligan
Nicolas Mills
Tina Muller
Peter Murray
Robin Nicholson
Olivia Noel
Kaori Ohsugi
Tony O'Neil
Monica Ors
Ana Otero
Elizabeth Page
Rawden Pettitt
Juliet Phillips
Jeremy Pitts
Venetia Playne
Tatiana von Preussen
Oliver Ralphs
Sandy Rendel
Patrick Richard
Wendy Robin
Bert Rozeman
Claudia Schmidek
Ryan Schmidt
Juliette Searight
Anwar Selleh
Tom Shell
Steven Shorter
Chris Smith
John Southall

Alan Stanton
Poppy Stanton
Thea Stanton
Caryl Stephen
Tammy Storey
Alex Street
Mary Sweeting
Zoe Symonds
Vera Tang
Fernando Tapia
Michele Tarroni
Gary Taylor
Stephen Taylor
Moritz Thierfelder
Paula Trindade
Ian Troake
Daniel Tsoi
Gary Turnbull
Tom Verebes
Ben Vickery
Richard Wardle
David Wares
James Wells
Ben Williams
Henry Williams
Paul Williams
Tess Williams
Yvonne Williams
Alain Wolff
Sarah Wong
Reiko Yamazaki
Carmen Nga Man Yip
Kern Young
Laura Young

Clients

A&D Properties
Argent Group
Artakt
Arts Council of Great Britain
Ashmolean Museum, Oxford
Baylight Properties
Belgrade Theatre Trust
Berkeley Homes
Bildurn Properties
Birchall Properties
Birkbeck College, University of London
Birmingham City Council
Blackpool Council
British Council
British Museum
Britten–Pears Foundation
Brunel University
Cadbury
Chester University College
City University
Classic FM
Clore Duffield Foundation
Compton Verney House Trust
Cranfield University
Crawley Borough Council
Crest Nicholson
Derwent London
Design Museum, London
Dorrington Properties
Drivers Jonas
Ebury Securities
English Heritage
Findon Holdings
Focus Consultants
Gatsby Charitable Foundation
Greater London Authority
Grosvenor Estates
Guildhall School of Music
Hammerson
Hayward Gallery
Headley Trust
Historic Royal Palaces
ING Real Estate Development
International House
Issey Miyake International
King Edward VI School, Chelmsford
Land Securities
Landmark Trust
Lincoln College, Oxford University
London Borough of Brent
London Borough of Camden
London Borough of Hackney
London Borough of Havering
London Development Agency
London Underground Limited
Lordland Europe
Marks & Spencer
Metro Imaging
Mountgrange
Museum of Modern Art, Oxford
National Film & Television School
National Gallery
National Maritime Museum
National Portrait Gallery
National Trust
Olympic Delivery Authority
Osho International
Rother District Council

Royal Academy
Royal Borough of Kensington & Chelsea
Royal Botanic Gardens, Kew
Royal Fine Arts Society
Royal Institute of British Architects
Royal National Theatre
Royal Observatory, Greenwich
Royal Society of Arts
Selfridges & Co
Senatsverwaltung fur Stadtentwicklung, Berlin
Soros Foundation
South Bank Board
South London Gallery
St George-in-the-East Trust
Stadt Königswinter
Tate Gallery
Thornfield Properties
Transport for London
Truro Cathedral
Turnberry Consulting
Università di Padova
University of Brighton
University of Cambridge
University of the Arts London
Victoria & Albert Museum
Ville de Genève
Wartski
Warwickshire County Council
Westminster Abbey
Whistles
Wiltshire County Council
Winchester Cathedral

Awards

Bournville Place, Birmingham
2009 RIBA West Midlands Award
2009 Civic Trust Award
2009 British Council of Offices Award,
Midlands & East Anglia Award
for Corporate Workplace

Department Store, Bristol
2009 RIBA Wessex Award

Cranfield University Accommodation, Bedfordshire
2009 Civic Trust Award
2009 Times Education Leadership
and Management Awards,
Outstanding New Student
Residence Award

Belgrade Theatre, Coventry
2008 RIBA National Award
2008 RIBA West Midlands Award
2008 D&AD Award
2008 Finalist for Civic Trust Award

University of the Arts London, King's Cross
2008 Commended, MIPIM Architectural
Review Future Project Award

Tower Hill, The Tower of London
2006 Finalist, VI European Prize for Urban
Public Space
2006 Natural Stone Landscaping Award
2005 RIBA London and English Heritage
Award for a Building in an
Historic Context
2005 Royal Fine Arts Trust Building of the
Year Award—Creating a
Beautiful Space
2005 RIBA London Urban Space by
Design Award
2005 RIBA London Building of the Year
2005 RIBA Award
2005 Structural Steel Design Award
2005 The Green Apple Award for the
Built Environment &
Architectural Heritage
2005 IStructE Structural Heritage Award
2004 Highly Commended, Europa
Nostra Awards

Compton Verney Art Gallery, Warwickshire
2006 Excellence in England Small Visitor
Attraction of the Year
2005 Civic Trust Award
2005 Civic Trust Special Award for
Culture & Regeneration
2004 RIBA Award
2004 Finalist, Royal Fine Arts Trust Building
of the Year Award
1998 Celebration of Excellence in
Design Award, Stratford-on-Avon
District Council
1997 Stone Federation Award

Rainham Village Urban Design Framework, London
2005 Finalist, RIBA London Urban Space
by Design Award

Casa Fontana, Lugano Switzerland
2004 RIBA Worldwide Award

Whitby Abbey Headland Project, Yorkshire
2003 Europa Nostra Award
2003 RIBA Award
2003 Civic Trust Award
2002 RIBA White Rose Award
2002 RICS Award

Selfridges, Manchester Central
2003 Department Store Interior of the
Year Award

Wellcome Trust Millennium Building, West Sussex
2001 RIBA Award
2001 Finalist, Design Sense
Sustainable Award
2001 Concrete Society Award
2001 West Sussex Heritage
Millennium Award
2001 Finalist, Royal Fine Arts Trust Building
of the Year Award
2000 Civic Trust Award

4 Brindleyplace, Birmingham
2000 Best of the Best, British Council
of Offices Award
1999 Regional, National and Best of
Best Award for Commercial
Workplace Building Category
Built in Quality Award

60 Sloane Avenue, London
1997 British Council of Offices Award
1996 Civic Trust Award
1996 RIBA Award
1995 Royal Borough of Kensington
and Chelsea Design Award

Issey Miyake, London
1991 D&AD Silver Award
1988 D&AD Gold Award

Old Royal Observatory, Greenwich
1995 Europa Nostra Award
1994 National Heritage Award

Gas Hall, Birmingham
1994 RIBA Award

Triforium Gallery, Winchester Cathedral
1992 Museum of the Year Award

Design Museum, London
1990 Civic Trust Award

Project Information

Issey Miyake Men
Client: Issey Miyake UK Limited
Location: Brompton Road, London, UK
Date of Completion: 1987

Main Contractor: Howard &
   Constable Partnership
Structural Engineer: Ove Arup & Partners
Services Engineer: George Buxton
   (electrical services)
Quantity Surveyor: Hanscomb
   Partnership
Lighting Consultants: John Johnson,
   Ace McLaren

Issey Miyake Women
Client: Issey Miyake UK Limited
Location: Brompton Road, London, UK
Date of Completion: 1988

Main Contractor: Howard &
   Constable Contracts
Structural Engineer: Nickalls & Roche
Services Engineer: N E Inglis & Partners
Lighting Consultants: Ace McCarron
Installations: Sally Greaves Lord
Quantity Surveyor: Stockdale

Issey Miyake Pleats Please
Client: Issey Miyake UK Limited
Location: Brook Street, London, UK
Date of Completion: 1996

Main Contractor: Shinn & Stetford
Structural Engineer: Michael
   Chester Associates
Services Engineer: Michael
   Popper Associates
Lighting Consultants: Lightwaves
Quantity Surveyor: Stockdale

Issey Miyake Women
Client: Issey Miyake UK Limited
Location: Conduit Street, London, UK
Date of Completion: 1999

Main Contractor: Pat Carter
   Contracts Limited
Structural Engineer: Greig Ling
Services Engineer: Buro Happold
Other Consultants: MCE
Quantity Surveyor: Stockdale
Lighting Designer: Ingo Maurer
Retail Property Consultant: Phillipa Jeal
Site Engineering: SES/ESL

Compton Verney Art Gallery
Client: Compton Verney House Trust
Location: Warwickshire, UK

Phase I
Date of Completion: 1998
Conservation Architect: Rodney Melville
   & Partners
Management Contractor: Bovis
Structural Engineer: Gifford & Partners
Services Engineer: Oscar Faber
Landscape Architect: Cass Associates
Traffic Consultant: Oscar Faber TPA
Quantity Surveyor: Davis Langdon
   and Everest
Client Representative: Jim O'Donahue

Phase II
Date of Completion: 2004
Conservation Architect: Rodney
   Melville & Partners
Main Contractor: Linford Group
Structural Engineer: Gifford & Partners
Services Engineer, Planning Supervision:
   FaberMaunsell
Landscape Architect: Colvin
   and Moggridge
Lighting Consultant: LAPD
Roads & Traffic Consultant: WA Fairhurst
   & Partners
Security Consultants: Consort Securities
Quantity Surveyor, Project Manager: John
   Austin & Partners
Exhibition Designer: Metaphor with
   Stanton Williams

Casa Fontana
Client: Confidential
Location: Lugano, Switzerland
Date of Completion: 2000

Site Architect: Otto + Associati SA
Structural Engineer: Regolati e Spadea SA
Mechanical Engineer: Verilux SA
Electrical Engineer: Atel Elettroimpianti
Pool Engineer: Idrosun SA
Interior Design: Stanton Williams with
   Shideh Shaygan
Project Manager: Peter Steger

Wellcome Trust Millennium Building
Client: Trustees Royal Botanic
   Gardens Kew
Location: Wakehurst Place, West Sussex, UK
Date of Completion: 2000

Main Contractor: James Langley
Structural Engineer: Michael
   Barclay Partnership
Services Engineer: Pearce
   Buckle Partnership
Environmental Assessment: EA Planning,
Environmental and development
   Consultancy
Fire Safety/Building Regs: BRCS
Planning Supervisor: PFB Construction
   Management
Exhibition Design: Land Design with
   Stanton Williams
Quantity Surveyor: Gordon Fanshaw
   & Partners
Management Consultant:
   Hornagold & Hills

Tower Hill
Client: Historic Royal Palaces
Location: Tower of London, UK
Date of Completion: 2004

Structural Engineer: Arup
Services Engineer: Arup
Quantity Surveyor: Gardiner and Theobold
Main Contractor: Wallis
Soft Landscape Consultants: Churchman
   Landscape Architects
Fire Engineer: Arup Fire
Planning Consultant: Hannah, Reed
   & Associates

Archaeological Consultant: Keevil
   Heritage Consultancy
Lighting Consultant: LAPD
Traffic Consultant: Pell Frischman
   Consultants

Belgrade Theatre
Client: Belgrade Theatre Trust
Location: Coventry, UK
Date of Completion: 2007

Main Contractor Phase A: Galliford Try
Main Contractor Phase B: ISG Interior
   Exterior
Structural Engineer: Flint and
   Neil Partnership
Services Engineer: RYB Konsult
Theatre Consultant: Theatreplan
Acoustic Consultant: Arup Acoustics
Access Consultant: All Clear Design
Fire Engineer: Faber Maunsell
Building Control: Approved Inspectors
Planning Supervisor: Quoin Consultancy
Quantity Surveyor: Davis Langdon
Project Manager: Buro Four
   Project Services

Department Store
Client: The Bristol Alliance—Hammerson
   and Land Securities
Location: Cabot Circus, Bristol, UK
Date of Completion: 2008

Main Contractor: Sir Robert McAlpine
Structural Engineer: Waterman Partnership
Services Engineer: Hoare Lea
Facade Engineer: Arup Façade
   Engineering
Quantity Surveyor: Cyril Sweett
Artist: Susanna Heron
Public Art Consultant: Insite Arts
Fit-out architects: Kinnersley Kent Design

Contributors

Ken Arnold
Staging a Thought

Ken has worked in a variety of museums on both sides of the Atlantic. He joined the Wellcome Trust in 1992 and now directs the events and exhibitions presented at the Wellcome Collection (a young venue that explores the links between medicine, life and art). He regularly writes and lectures on museums and on contemporary relations between the arts and sciences.

Stephen Bayley
In the end, it's all about this

Over 30 years his books and articles and exhibitions have changed people's perception of design. In 1989 he opened London's Design Museum whose exhibition space was designed by Stanton Williams. He was one of their very first clients.

Alistair Fair
Project Descriptions

Alistair is an architectural historian and writer with interests in buildings from the Renaissance to the present and a PhD on twentieth century British theatre architecture. He recently completed a detailed account of Stanton Williams' work at the Belgrade Theatre which will appear in a forthcoming study of contemporary British arts buildings.

Irénée Scalbert
Starting at the Beginning
A Pure Space

Irénée is an architecture critic and historian. He has taught at the Architectural Association where he co-ordinated the History and Theory Programme, and at the Graduate School of Design at Harvard as a Visiting Design Critic. He presently teaches at the School of Architecture, University of Limerick in Ireland and lives in London.

David Taylor
Alan Stanton and Paul Williams in Conversation

David is a freelance journalist and author. A former acting editor of *The Architects' Journal,* he currently edits the *London Property Review,* has written for various newspapers and magazines, produced exhibitions at the New London Architecture Gallery, was on CABE's writers' panel for four years and has contributed chapters to books including *Architecture and Commerce—New Office Design in London* and *1000 Buildings You Must See Before You Die.* He lives in Brighton with his wife and two children.

Acknowledgements

It is perhaps a truism that an architectural project is only as good as its client. However we remain extremely grateful to all our clients who have given us the opportunities to work on a wide range of fascinating projects. For their faith in us and the support shown in our early days, we owe a special debt to Maureen Doherty, Val Archer and Crispin Kelly, and of course the wonderful Hayward Gallery team led by the late Joanna Drew.

It is also true that architecture is a collaborative activity and we would like to recognise the creative and practical contributions made by engineers, specialist consultants, makers and builders to our built work.

As directors we have had the good fortune to work with very talented people at Stanton Williams and recognise the massive input made by everyone, especially our associates and the studio team, as we have all struggled to 'raise the bar' and even sometimes to achieve the impossible.

In a sense, we have been constructing this book for years, and although perhaps it could never fulfil our aspirations completely, it would not have happened without Stuart Bourne here in the studio, whose patient tenacity has held the project together.

Finally our thanks must go to our families for their invaluable support, encouragement and inspiration.

Image Credits

Black Dog Publishing Limited
10A Acton Street
London
WC1X 9NG

t.   +44 (0)207 713 5097
f.   +44 (0)207 713 8682
e.   info@blackdogonline.com

Designed by Cartlidge Levene

Project Manager/Design Direction: Stuart Bourne

Stanton Williams
36 Graham Street
London, N1 8GJ
Phone +44 (0)20 7880 6400
Email info@stantonwilliams.com
www.stantonwilliams.com

British Library Cataloguing-in-Publication Data.
A CIP record for this book is available from the British Library.

ISBN 978 1 906155 87 2

Black Dog Publishing is an environmentally responsible
company. *Volume—Stanton Williams* is printed on FSC
certified Garda Matt 170 gsm paper.

architecture art design
fashion history photography
theory and things

www.blackdogonline.com